WHISKEY MASTER CLASS

THE ULTIMATE GUIDE TO UNDERSTANDING
SCOTCH, BOURBON, RYE, AND MORE

—— LEW BRYSON ——

HARVARD
COMMON
PRESS

Brimming with creative inspiration, how-to projects, and useful information to enrich your everyday life, Quarto Knows is a favorite destination for those pursuing their interests and passions. Visit our site and dig deeper with our books into your area of interest: Quarto Creates, Quarto Cooks, Quarto Homes, Quarto Lives, Quarto Drives, Quarto Explores, Quarto Gifts, or Quarto Kids.

Design: www.traffic-design.co.uk

Cover Illustration: www.shutterstock.com

Page Layout: www.traffic-design.co.uk

Photography: Jack Sorokin Photography: pages 8, 12, 21, 22, 24, 31, 37, 60, 64, 72, 74, 79, 82, 86, 98, 100, 103, 111, 114, 121, 123, 126, 130, 140, 146, 150, 157, 163, 168, 179, 186, 196, 198, 203, 205, 206, 211, 220, 226, 237, 238, 242, 244; Courtesy of the author: pages 13, 15, 41, 44, 62, 71, 83, 93, 95, 106, 109, 112, 119, 129, 133, 138, 141, 145, 153, 161, 162, 167, 181, 183, 191, 212, 223, 231, 400; Shutterstock: pages 6, 17, 46, 50, 53, 55, 56, 58, 63, 67, 85, 88, 105, 149, 184, 209, 234

Printed in China

FOREWORD

Over the years, there have been many books written on whiskey—either spelled with an e or not. A lot of these books have been very, very good and proven to be superb introductions for learning about whiskies, especially for beginners new to the subject. Indeed, in my student days at Heriot Watt University, in Edinburgh, I borrowed many of these tomes myself; I even bought a few of them! Many people have enjoyed reading the details of how whiskey is distilled, where the distilleries are located, and they've loved the often-beautiful photographs and illustrations that accompany these words—helping to bring the entire subject to life.

If one embarks on a career in the global whiskey industry or becomes much more knowledgeable about the subject through numerous tastings, masterclasses, seminars, and in-depth study, you inevitably reach a stage where to progress there are only two options really. Either you spend many years actually making the stuff, or you find a document or book that covers things in lovely, geeky scientific detail. I hadn't really seen anything that gets close to the latter until now.

I have had the pleasure of knowing and interacting with Lew for many years now, and I have always thoroughly enjoyed the sometimes challenging, but always thought-provoking and enjoyable, debates I have had with him. In addition to his encyclopedic knowledge of the waters of life in all their various forms, Lew also has a certain sense of humor, which has helped us to bond and forge a great working relationship. So, it is with great pleasure that I have written this brief foreword to what I am certain will become an absolute must-have for any students of whiskey, either for business or pleasure. When I first saw the draft contents for Whiskey Master Class, I genuinely thought, "At last, this is the one." So, happy learning everyone!

WᴅL

Dr Bill Lumsden

Director of Distilling,
Whisky Creation & Whisky Stocks
Glenmorangie & Ardbeg

Contents

The Syllabus

Chapter 1:

What do you taste… what do you smell when you take a sip of whiskey? If it's Scotch, you may taste tar or dried fruit or marmalade. Trying a bourbon? Scents of maple or blackberry or coconut come from the glass. Irish? A lush selection of fruit, maybe a grassy freshness. Sipping a Canadian might yield caramel, roasted nuts, and a zippy note of spice. Japanese can offer a bosky note of greenery, perhaps smoky plum notes. Grab a small distillery whiskey and anything's on the table: barbecue, hot tires, strawberries, peanuts, or peppermint.

All of these flavors are different, and these whiskey traditions are singular enough that you can often tell what you're drinking just by the flavors and aromas. But all these flavors and aromas also have something in common: Not one of them is an ingredient in the whiskey. No blackberries, no peanuts, no marmalade, and certainly no tires have been added!

Then where do they come from? The answer to that question is found in the answer to the larger questions: What is whiskey, and how is it made? There are flavors and aromas being made (or taken away) at every step, and every step is necessary to the way the whiskey tastes.

One of the jobs of a whiskey writer is tasting whiskey and then describing it to readers. Writers speak of "teasing apart" the aromas to figure out what is in there, a process of deconstructing the whiskey, figuring out what went into it and how it was made.

That's what the book is about. It's about how whiskey makers go about creating, building, and integrating flavor.

Whiskey or Whisky?

*One of the biggest arguments about whiskey is how
to spell it. It's generally "whiskey" in America (though
Maker's Mark, Old Forester, and George Dickel drop
the "e") and Ireland, while it's "whisky" in Scotland,
Canada, and Japan. (You can remember it easily:
Ireland and America both have an "e" in them; the
other countries don't.) The other small producers in
various countries do as they see fit, though it's most
often "whisky."*

There is no argument. "Whisky" and "whiskey" are pronounced the same, and they mean the same thing. It's like the difference between "aluminum" in America and "aluminium" in Canada: a letter, nothing else. The differences are all in how the spirit in question is made, which we'll examine in chapter 2.

I'll be using "whiskey" unless I'm talking specifically about Scotch, Canadian, or Japanese whiskies. The only reason why is because I'm writing this in America. Really, it's just spelling.

Some of this will be things you already know. Even thirty years ago, informed whiskey drinkers would have known the difference between a blended Scotch and a single malt, though they may or may not have actually understood just what "malt" is. They probably knew that whiskey was aged in oak barrels, though they may not have known what kind, or why, or what that did to the whiskey.

They knew that whiskey was made with a still, and they probably had a vague idea of how a pot still

worked. Very few of them had ever been to a distillery; very few distilleries offered tours.

Today's whiskey drinkers are much more sophisticated, more engaged. They want to know all they can about their chosen drink. "Transparency" is their watchword. They want to know where the whiskey is made and go there to see it being made. Tell us, they ask, what grains are being used, where they are from, and in what ratios they are included. Don't stop there: Tell us what yeast is used, how the mash is made, and maybe even what kind of fermentation vessel is used. Then they want to know more about the still: what kind it is, how it is shaped, and how the distillation is done. Take them in the cooperage and show them the barrels. Take them to the warehouse; they must see how it is constructed and where it is sited.

But unless you're in the industry, or you're a dedicated whiskey writer like me, or you're an exceptionally well-read, well-traveled whiskey drinker, I can almost guarantee you'll find things in this book you don't know—things that are new to you.

It might be the components of water chemistry, the thermal path of fermentation, the history and chemistry of sour mash, or the intricacies of Scottish still design. It might be the influence of the design and position of the warehouse, the size and shape of the barrel, or the climate where the whiskey is aged. Maybe it's something as simple but easily misunderstood as the concept of "blended whiskey."

Or maybe—and this was one of the main reasons that I wrote the book— maybe for you it's the forest and not the trees. I find that in whiskey appreciation, as is the case in many a hobbyist's interest, people tend to put a heavy emphasis on one or two factors that they find particularly interesting or simply easier to grasp.

Bourbon aficionados may obsess over the mashbill, the ratio of the different grains that make up the whiskey's formulation. Scotch drinkers may only care about the parts per million of phenol, a numeric measure of smoke content. Irish drinkers want to know if a whiskey is a single pot still type or what kind of barrels were used. Canadian drinkers want to know the rye content and what's in the bottle besides whisky. Japanese whisky aficionados, the poor devils, are just trying to find a bottle as the industry scrambles to catch up with demand. And craft whiskey drinkers are usually focused on location, location, location.

All of those things are important. But none of them are the be-all and end-all of how those whiskeys taste. You need to keep your eye on the big picture, the whole process. As renowned Scotch whisky blender Dr. Bill Lumsden says, "If the barrel gives a whisky 50 percent of its flavor . . . that just means that the other 50 percent *doesn't* come from the barrel." To really understand a whiskey, you have to know where every bit of that 100 percent comes from and how it's different from another whiskey.

What Is Whiskey?

*To understand **that**, we should talk briefly about what is whiskey and what isn't.*

In the simplest terms, whiskey is a drink made from fermented grain that is then distilled and aged in wooden barrels. But it turns out that "the simplest terms" can get you in trouble. For instance, in the United States, the regulations don't put any minimum on the amount of time that is considered aging. In Canada, Ireland, and Scotland, the spirit has to be in the barrel for at least three years before it can be called "whiskey" (or "whisky"). There are limits on the percentage alcohol of the spirit coming off the final distillation: some as low as 80 percent, some as high as 95 percent.

You can depend on the basics. Although there are other spirits in the world that are called "whiskey," particularly in south Asia, they are made wholly or partly from nongrain fermentables, like sugar, and are not generally considered to be whiskey outside of their home countries. There are unaged grain spirits that are distilled to a very high proof: We call them "vodka." Despite what people may tell you, there is no "potato whiskey" or "sugar whiskey." But if it's distilled from 100 percent grain and aged in wood, it's whiskey.

Touring the Buffalo Trace Distillery in Frankfort, Kentucky

How did that come to be whiskey? Mainly because in the late medieval period, when Arabic texts on the science of distillation collided with scholarly European monks who could read them, it was in the colder climes of Ireland (or maybe Scotland—it's not 100 percent certain). The most common source of alcohol for distilling there was beer, the drink of northern Europe. Whiskey, or *usquebaugh* as it was originally called in Gaelic (pronounced, roughly, "ish-ka b'ah"), found a foothold among the monks of Ireland and Scotland and eventually spread to small farmers.

While distilling got big in the Lowlands and the towns of Scotland and Ireland, up in the hills the Scottish farmers continued working away on their small copper pot stills. This would become the basis for single malt Scotch whisky, once they started aging it in used barrels. It wasn't exactly legal, but it was easier than selling grain. It took eight mules to carry the grain used to make one mule-load of whiskey, and the whiskey was worth more. Once legal distilling became possible, an industry was born.

Distilling in the New World took root after the immigration of Scots-Irish and German distillers. Germans had a tradition of grain spirit made largely from rye. The rye whiskey makers in Pennsylvania, and later the distillers who developed bourbon in Kentucky, were largely German. The man George Washington hired to run his rye whiskey distillery at Mount Vernon after the Revolutionary War, though, was a Scotsman. Canadian distillers were largely Scottish and English.

Whiskey took hold as a good drink, a nonperishable drink, unlike beer and wine. It had a better reputation than gin, and when the phylloxera aphids struck the French cognac industry, thirsty Britons turned to their native drink, whiskey, and found it good. One hundred and twenty years ago, whiskey was the dominant spirit of the Western world. As Japan came out of its self-imposed retreat in the late 1800s, they too discovered Scotch whisky and liked it so much that they would develop their own distinctive malt and blended whiskies.

That's how it would remain until the 1960s, with the rise of vodka and light rum. Whiskey sales fell, and by the 1980s there was a glut of Scotch whisky, and distilleries were closing. Whisky makers turned to single malts as a way to sell some of that unwanted whisky and discovered that the more flavorful, more expensive whiskies were quite popular with the right customers. Bourbon and Irish distillers followed the same path of premiumization to success in the first decade of the twenty-first century.

Perhaps the greatest signal of whiskey's return to glory is the way the new small distillers have embraced it. Well over eighteen hundred of these craft distillers were open in America in 2018, with hundreds more around the world. More than half of them are making whiskey, and they're making whiskey in a robust number of varieties, some in tribute to forgotten styles that haven't been made in more than one hundred years, some in ways that have surely never been seen before.

Whiskey is a great story. Now learn the rest of it: how it's made.

Making Whiskey

Making whiskey, even average whiskey, is about flavor creation and flavor control; and there are a lot of different ways to do it. Each of the "Big Five" whiskey regions has different ways of going about making a good whiskey; the new craft distillers, as you might expect, have a wide variety of ways to do it. All of those ways rely on putting together a varied mix of elements from four categories.

Moonshine

You have probably heard of moonshine, the colloquial name for illegally made (and therefore untaxed) spirits. They are usually unaged and not made from all grain: Corn sugar is a common shortcut. Some are better than others, and you may hear stories about moonshine that is "finer than store-bought whiskey."

Real Moonshine

Unaged, unnamed, untaxed, illegal: the real thing, from central Pennsylvania. Clear, smelling sharply of alcohol and sugar. Hot, a bit rough, cornmeal sweet, short hot finish, surprisingly clean.

Pardon my French, but poppycock. Moonshiners may take pride in their product, but they're not doing any more than they have to, to be slightly better than their local competition. No one makes 'shine for the purpose of making fine whiskey; they do it to make some relatively easy money. Thanks to the high taxes on spirits in many countries, illicit distillation can be a profitable sideline, if you can keep it hidden.

And you have to keep it hidden pretty well, because if you get caught, it's a large fine plus jail time. It doesn't matter if you're "only making it for friends." If you make spirits without a license in the United States and most countries (except New Zealand), you are committing a crime.

What about the bottles of "moonshine" you see on store shelves, usually flavored with fruit or spices (or artificial flavorings)? That's a catch-22: They're legal because they're licensed; but because they're legal, they're not really moonshine. That's part of its very definition: It's called moonshine because it's made by the light of the moon, under the cover of darkness, because if you get caught, it's the hoosegow for you. "Legal moonshine" is an oxymoron, like "deafening silence."

What's interesting is that those flavorings are a callback to the way whiskey was made back in the very dawn of distilled spirits. Flavorings were added

MOONSHINE

because distillation was such an arcane process, the spirits were often made palatable only by the additions.

My advice?

Stick to store-bought.

A small, crude moonshine still

MOONSHINE

The four categories are *the material, the process, the environment,* and *the people.*

Material is the actual things that go into making whiskey: grain, water, yeast (and bacteria), yeast nutrients, copper, barrels, and sometimes a bit of caramel.

Process is what gets done to the materials. Grain is malted, sprouted, and then heated to kill the sprout. It is milled, then hydrated and cooked in a process called mashing (followed by lautering, filtering the grain out, unless it's in America). Then it's fermentation, followed directly by distillation. The spirit is cut to entry proof and barreled prior to months or years of aging. The whiskey may be finished in a different barrel. It's then dumped, filtered, and proofed before bottling.

Environment is more subtle. It's what's around the whiskey from start to finish. It's the climate the trees and grain grew in, the weather that stoked the draft of the malthouse, or the heat and cool of the warehouse. Altitude is becoming more and more important as distilleries pop up along slopes. It's the location, the terroir, of the distillery and the warehouses.

Finally, *people* make the whiskey, putting experience and attention into it. Here's how it happens.

Whiskey is an agricultural product. It starts in the fields. Grain is grown and harvested, and then evaluated.

Grain fit for distilling is top-quality stuff, be it barley, corn, wheat, rye, or anything else. It must be free of rot, have the right levels of protein and nitrogen, the right moisture content, and most importantly, it has to smell clean and right.

The grain must be cleaned and processed. For barley, that usually means *malting*, forcing the grain to sprout before heating it to kill the sprout. This causes the creation of *enzymes* that will transform starches to sugars as the grain or grains that go into the whiskey are carefully cooked, or *mashed*. The cooking makes that transformation happen by breaking loose the starches in the grains and allowing the enzymes to chemically transform them. The enzymes work best at specific temperature ranges, so this part requires careful control.

Now the mash, a thin cereal porridge full of sugars, is cooled and is either pumped directly to fermentation tanks (in the case of American whiskeys) or has the solids strained out first. Yeast is added, and fermentation begins. The yeast attacks the sugars and consumes them, creating alcohol, carbon dioxide, and a variety of flavor and aroma compounds.

The resulting *distiller's beer* (still containing grains), or *wash* (strained liquid), goes to the still.

If it's a pot still, it is *charged* with a capacity load of wash and heated until the alcohol starts to vaporize.

Alcohol vaporizes at a lower temperature than water, which is how distillation creates spirits. The first distillation, in the *wash still*, gets rid of a lot of the water. The second distillation, in the *spirit still*, is about *cutting* the spirit run to capture its alcohol heart.

There are compounds other than alcohol that vaporize at those lower temperatures that aren't desirable, referred to as *heads* or *foreshots*. Those are allowed to be cooked off first, before the distiller makes the first *cut* and starts collecting the cleaner alcohol vapors and desirable aromatics (the *hearts*) in usable amounts. The vapors are captured until they peter out and other undesirable compounds start to join them in moving up the still, the *tails* or *feints*. The second cut is made, and this is also put aside. Some of the set-aside cuts will be redistilled to recover all the alcohol; eventually, the leftovers will be disposed of (often burned for heat). There may be an additional distillation (common in Irish whiskey) to further "clean" the spirit.

In a beer still (or "stripper still"), a continuous flow of beer enters the column, dropping down through a series of perforated plates, while live steam makes its way up through the same plates.

As the alcohol is heated, it's stripped out of the beer and rises near the top, where it is collected and sent to a condenser. The leftover beer, still containing the grain solids and dead yeast, drains to the bottom; and in bourbon and American rye, a portion is usually sent back to the fermenters as *sour mash* to feed the yeast and set the optimal pH level of the mash.

Another type of column still, known as a Coffey still, runs on wash and has two columns. It distills to a much higher proof and is a bit more complicated to explain; we'll save that for chapter 8 (page 114). For now, all we need to know is that it is usually used for making grain whiskey for blending.

The new make, the just-distilled spirit, is clear as water and smells mainly of the sweetness of the grain, accentuated by the sweetness of the alcohol. Now it is *proofed*, where water is slowly added to bring it down to the proof, or percentage of alcohol desired for barreling. The proofed spirit is poured into a barrel. The barrel may be a new charred white oak barrel (used for American whiskeys, and sparingly in some others) or a used oak barrel that once held other whiskey or wine or a fortified wine, like sherry or port. The barrel is closed with a wooden or plastic plug, called a *bung*, and stood in a warehouse to age.

Over the next however many years, the whiskey will push into the wood as the summer heat makes it expand and pull back out as the cold of winter makes it contract.

The warehouse may be heated and cooled to create that effect on a more rapid, consistent basis. The spirit is extracting color, flavor, and aroma from the wood; and the layer of char is filtering undesirable flavors and aromas out of the spirit. The blender, the warehouse manager, and the distiller will keep tabs on the barrels, tasting them over the years to see how they are developing.

When the whiskey is ready, properly aged and tasting the way it should for the style that's being made from it, the barrel is removed from the warehouse and *dumped*. It may be only lightly filtered to remove any bits of barrel char or chilled and more tightly filtered to prevent any protein haziness in your bottle or glass. Some whiskeys are allowed by regulation to have caramel coloring added at this point; others are not. The coloring is made from the same grain as the whiskey and is added for visual consistency.

The whiskey may be blended with other barrels at this time, or it may go for a single-cask bottling. Once the desired flavor and character are achieved and the blender or distiller is satisfied, the whiskey is proofed to bottling strength (or left as it came from the barrel, for a cask-strength whiskey). Now it is bottled, labeled, boxed, shipped, and sold, perhaps to you or me.

That's how whiskey is made. It is a product that is a result of natural ingredients like grain and water; processes like fermentation and distillation; chemical and physical interactions with oak over a number of years; and decisions made by human beings all along the way.

Whiskey flavor doesn't come from any single place. There are sources that have more effect than others— the barrel, the grain, the yeast, for example—but there are many, many things that contribute to the final totality that is each bottle of whiskey, and the next, and the next.

It doesn't matter if it's a \$12 bottle from the bottom shelf or a \$12,000 bottle locked and chained in a display cabinet. It's still materials, process, environment, and the people who put them together. Is water a minor source of flavor? It's a major part of the whiskey, and you can't mash or ferment without it. Does it matter if the barrel is in a warehouse on the sea or 20 miles (32.2 km) inland? Rates of evaporation say it does. Does it matter where the peat for your malting was dug? Spectral analysis proves that it does.

Understanding these flavor-creation inputs is the key to understanding whiskey. When you learn them, you can talk about whiskey in a more informed way and ask questions from a more informed vantage. You're more likely to understand the answers, too.

The importance of the building blocks of flavor is not equal. Neither is it absolute, because their importance depends on the whiskey being created. Yeast is crucial to every whiskey, but particularly to whiskeys with rye in the mash, because what yeast is used determines the amount of rye "spiciness" that will be expressed. The uniformity of the new, charred oak barrel is important to bourbon, but the type of used barrel a Scotch (or Irish, Canadian, or Japanese) whisky goes into means there is more variety possible in the final flavor. The type of grain is important to a craft distiller because it can represent a critical advantage and point of difference.

None of the ingredients or processes are unimportant; all must be considered. From the type of barrel and the time spent in it, to the temperature of the fermentation and the shape of the still, down to where the oak for the barrel grew and the weather on the day the grain was harvested, whiskey is solid proof of the butterfly effect. That's what makes it wonderful. There are always new whiskeys waiting to be made.

If you're ready, let's start taking this stuff apart, piece by piece. We'll start with the rules, the regulations, traditions, and expectations that make up the Big Five separate whiskey regions, and the wild innovation that characterizes the new craft distillers. And then, we'll make some whiskey.

Frozen yeast samples at Wilderness Trail Distillery (Danville, KY)

The Whiskeys

There are five major whiskey regions in the world: Scotland, Ireland, Canada, America, and Japan. The traditional whiskey makers, the "legacy" distillers as some call them, are found there. The names and the whiskeys are among the more familiar. Many of these distillers have grown in size recently—some quite strikingly—as whiskey sales have increased strongly. They have also been joined by new, small distillers. The total numbers range from a handful in Canada, Ireland, and Japan to more than 100 in Scotland. America has exploded, with well over 1,000 distillers now making spirits, many of them making whiskey.

What about the rest of the world? There are some distillers in Australia, and those have also grown recently in size and number. Over the past twenty years or so, new whiskey makers have been popping up across Europe, in South Africa, India, and Taiwan. Many of them are making malt whiskeys, more or less in imitation of, or homage to, Scotch; but they come with their own twists.

The thing to remember, of course, is that all whiskeys are very similar at their heart. As we discussed, they are all fermented grain beverages that have been distilled and then aged in wooden barrels. The differences come from the grain, the mashing and fermentation, the distillation, aging, and then the selection of barrels for bottling.

The major whiskey regions represent areas where a tradition of whiskey making has led to an identity, a set of similarities in the whiskeys from those regions. Every whiskey is still different, but within these regions, the whiskeys are more similar among themselves than to those from the other groups. The building blocks of flavor that we'll be addressing in this chapter are largely based on traditions and regulations. There are guidelines and rules for making whiskey, and they vary—sometimes by quite a bit—depending on where the whiskey is being made. Staying within those guidelines has a definite effect on the flavor of the whiskey.

The rest of the book is about differences. In this chapter, we'll talk about these regional similarities.

Scotch

The world dominance of Scotch whisky cannot be overstated. In 2018 there was more Scotch whisky sold worldwide than American, Canadian, and Irish whiskeys combined.

The large majority of those sales were well-known blended Scotch whisky brands: Johnnie Walker, Ballantine's, Grant's, Chivas Regal, J&B, Dewar's (and some that are not as well known in the United States, such as Label 5, William Lawson's, and William Peel). A lot of that is a direct result of English imperialism. Scotch whisky covered the world during the height of the British Empire. Ships flying the British flag (more than likely built and kept running by Scottish engineers) carried holds full of Scotch all over the globe, slaking the thirst of the British bureaucracy and military.

Even though the Empire has faded into dust, Scotch whisky endures and continues to conquer new territories. France is a huge market for Scotch, as is India, despite crushingly high import duties. The United States spends more on Scotch than any other country on Earth, even though we have excellent whiskeys of our own.

As whisky writer Dave Broom has said, "Scotch is how the world says 'whisky.'"

But what makes it Scotch? According to the Scotch Whisky Regulations of 2009, to be "Scotch Whisky" a spirit must hew to these standards. I've paraphrased the requirements in **boldface**, followed by an expansion on them.

1. Be mashed, fermented, distilled, and matured entirely in Scotland.

This simply states that the entire process of making the whisky, right up to before the bottling, has to take place *in Scotland*. Exceptions used to be made for partial aging in other countries, but no longer. The whisky may still be shipped in bulk and bottled in other countries.

2. Be made from water and malted barley ("to which only whole grains of other cereals may be added").

Two things to note here: That parenthetical part covers Scotch grain whisky, which is a blend of malt and other whole grains, often wheat. It also covers caramel coloring, which is made from malted barley wash, boiled down to a dark syrup for this purpose. Such coloring is allowed to be added, as we'll see below.

3. Be converted using only the enzymes in the grain.

Very traditional: No enzymes are allowed to be added to help the conversion of the grain's starches to sugars. This sets a minimum amount of malt that's required in grain whisky, but all-malt whisky

really has no need for any additional enzymes—the ones in the malt are more than sufficient.

4. Be fermented by the addition of only yeast.

No bacteria or other micro-organisms are allowed to be used. This is more restrictive than it sounds, as American and Japanese distillers may allow bacterial fermentation to create more flavor.

5. Be distilled to no more than 94.8 percent ABV.

This limit applies to the grain whiskies. Malt whisky is distilled to about 63 percent and must be distilled in pot stills, not columns.

6. Be matured in oak casks (maximum 700 liters [185 gallons]) in an excise ware house "or a permitted place" for no less than three years.

The part about the warehouse or "permitted place" is about taxes; the government wants to know where every drop is stored so they get every bit of the taxes they're owed. Oak is tradition and ensures a commonality of flavor, even though some of the oak was first used to age bourbon while other casks were used to age sherry or port. The size is the top end of the largest traditional casks (Madeira drums and port pipes). Even larger casks would presumably be cheaper to use but would have substantially less wood influence on the whisky.

7. Retain the color, aroma, and taste derived from the raw materials, process, and maturation.

"Don't change anything" is the watchword here. Chill filtration is allowed; that's a process that chills the whisky, causing proteins to precipitate, and then filters them out. Distillers do this so that if the whisky gets cold at some point in the supply chain, it won't become hazy and, thus, undesirable to the customer's eye. The process doesn't change the look of the unchilled whisky; whether it actually changes the "taste derived from..." is a question the industry has largely chosen to ignore.

---

8. Have nothing added to it other than water and/or "plain caramel coloring."

As noted earlier, this is caramel coloring made from the same "raw materials" as the whisky. Distillers may add small amounts of caramel coloring to make batches of whisky identical in color, as the color can vary depending on the casks used. The amount of caramel added is a point of some question (and occasional derision) among whisky aficionados, who suspect that some bottlings add so much that it changes the flavor. Older whiskies are often darker in color, so overadding caramel can make a whisky have an appearance that indicates more age.

9. Have a minimum alcohol by volume (ABV) of 40 percent.

This is about value, much like the standardized European Union/ United Kingdom bottle size of 700 ml. Drinkers want to know that the whisky is of at least a strength of 40 percent and bottled at a standard volume.

Is that the full definition of Scotch whisky? Yes and no. There are also five different types of Scotch, being a combination of the two basic types: malt and grain.

Single malt Scotch whisky is malt whisky that is all sourced from a single distillery.

Single grain Scotch whisky is grain whisky that is all sourced from a single distillery.

Blended Scotch whisky is a blend of one or more single malts and one or more single grains.

Blended malt Scotch whisky is a blend of two or more single malts, sourced from two or more distilleries.

Blended grain Scotch whisky is a blend of two or more single grains, sourced from two or more distilleries.

Haig Club is a blended grain whisky, designed to be an easy drink. Nose of toasted marshmallow and lightly cooked fruits. Creamy on the tongue, light oak outlines the big sweet pillow of warm marshmallow in the middle.

The flip side of blended Scotch whisky.

Of the five categories, blended Scotch whisky and single malt Scotch whisky are by far the largest in both numbers of brands and volume sold.

Now you know everything—and nothing—about Scotch whisky. Reading the regulations to understand the whisky is like describing the *Mona Lisa* as a portrait of a woman painted on wood with oil colors. I mean, we haven't even mentioned peat!

To understand the effect of the regulations, compare them to the rules of chess. They are not complicated; a child can master them in less than a week. That same child can play a game with an adult within a couple months. They may not win the game, but they will almost certainly make no mistakes within those simple rules. Those exact same rules, and the almost infinite opportunities for play and decisions within them, can form the stage for a brilliant game that challenges grand masters and the most advanced computers.

The Scotch Whisky Regulations are a fairly simple set of parameters for an industry that is following well-known processes that have been used for centuries. The rules are strict—page after page has been written about their restrictive nature and its effect on the industry—but they allow for both workaday production of a daily dram

at affordable prices and inspired works of genius that surpass the workaday level entirely. It's what a distiller does within those rules that makes that particular distiller's whisky different.

But what is it about the whiskies made under these regulations that make them uniquely Scotch whisky? Before you say "malt and pot stills," remember that blended Scotch whisky is partly other grains distilled in a column still, and nine out of ten bottles of Scotch whisky are blended (dollar sales are closer to three out of four for blended because of the higher price of single malts). It's clearly not peat smoke either, since many Scotch whiskies are made without the addition of so much as a breath of it. Is it used casks? It is not. Although used casks are traditional, there is nothing in the regulations that requires them; and there are a number of single malts and blends that are aged partially or entirely in new oak barrels. Remember also that Bushmills, fewer than 100 miles (160.9 km) from Scotland, makes a triple-distilled single malt in the same types of used barrels; and the Japanese whisky industry is based directly on that of Scotland, with only subtle, though significant, differences.

Just what is Scotch whisky? There has to be something more than a Justice Stewart–like pronouncement of "I know it when I taste it."

The obvious and easy answer is of Scotch whisky is whisky made entirely in Scotland, but that's cheating, really. It's more that it is whisky made by the Scotch whisky industry, within the traditions of that industry, because despite never-ending calls for breaking out of traditional restraints, Scotch whisky is a spirit of lasting, consistent character. Its DNA was developed by a combination of illicit Highland distillers making hefty malt whisky in small pot stills with a smoky peat "reek" and aged in used barrels as it was transported to market and commercial Lowland distillers who used more efficient, larger pot stills and the new column stills to make light grain whisky. Together they would make blends that many more people enjoyed than the product of either one separately.

Perhaps the heart of the Scotch Whisky Regulations and the heart of Scotch whisky is the part about retaining the color, aroma, and taste derived from the raw materials, process, and maturation—the parts that have evolved from those beginnings. Scotch is about reaching a point of satisfaction.

Even at its most extreme, the peat monster and sherry bomb single malts, or the most bland and inoffensive blends, Scotch whisky is about balance. Is there fiery, burnt peat? There is also the balm and sweetness of malt. Is there the barest hint of flavor in the bland mass-market blend, a wisp of smoke, a touch of sherry, a

mere smidgen of malt chewiness? Then there is nothing crashing on the opposite side of the scales to blast it away.

The Scotch whisky distillers have a saying: "Horses for courses." Just as you wouldn't run a quarter horse in a steeplechase, you wouldn't plunk ice in a fine single malt and douse it with soda. But that would be perfectly acceptable and expected with a blend.

The regulations may seem restrictive and overly prescriptive, but they are not so much restrictive as a recognition of the status quo. The distillers are already making this kind of whisky and have been for a long, long time. The regulations allow Scotch whisky to range from the swaggering stormy giants of Islay single malts to the lighthearted joyous dancers that are single grains and the solidly simple and loyal souls of the blends. All it takes to make the difference is ingredients, process, and human direction.

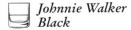

Johnnie Walker Black

My go-to when the chips are down on bar selection. Light smoke, spice, and citrus nose slides into firm wood smoke and sweet malt. Light but retaining authority enough to kick ice in a highball.

What about India?

When we're tossing around talk about the "biggest-selling whiskeys in the world," we're always talking about the whiskeys from the "traditional" whiskey-making areas, selling in the "traditional" whiskey-drinking areas, essentially Europe and North America, with a little attention paid to Japan: Johnnie Walker, Jim Beam, Jameson, Crown Royal, and Jack Daniel's.

What about the Indian whiskeys with much larger sales figures? McDowell's, Imperial Blue, and Royal Stag all have sales similar to, or larger than, Johnnie Walker. Officer's Choice is ranked as the biggest-selling whiskey in the world! This smacks of Eurocentrism of the worst kind.

If it is, it's about the Eurocentric definition of whisky as a drink distilled from grain and aged in wood. Indians do drink a lot of whiskey, undoubtedly a cultural imprint from the days of the Raj as much as the use of English as a second language. But most of the spirits made and sold in India as "whisky" are not recognized by most of the world's whisky markets as whisky. They are made largely with molasses and are considered closer to rum. They can be sold only in the European Union, for instance, if they are labeled as a "spirit drink."

Officer's Choice, which outsells Johnnie Walker by a factor of better than 3:2, is made with grain but is a blend of aged and unaged spirit. For the purposes of the whiskeys we're looking at here, I'm going to say it's not in the classification.

There are some excellent Indian malt whiskies. Amrut Distillery, Paul John, and a newcomer, Rampur Distillery, are all quite nice, very much in the style of Scotch whisky. But their fast aging and high evaporative losses (because of the climate) change the character and give them a subtle twist all their own. Keep an eye out and try them if you haven't had the chance.

Paul John Peated Select Cask

Carefully handled hot-climate aging brings out sweet malt through light peat smoke. On the palate, the smoke enlarges but doesn't overwhelm sweet, layered brown sugar and toffee, with a teasing note of dry cocoa.

Irish

Irish whiskey almost disappeared in the twentieth century. Sales in the 1970s were at their lowest point in many years. I remember those days, as they were when I was starting to drink.

I found the idea that Irish whiskey was at such a low point then to be crazy. I remembered bottles of Irish whiskey in almost every bar I went to back in those days. How could it be doing so badly? What didn't occur to me was that most of those bottles were the same ones that sat there from March 18 to March 15 of the following year. Irish whiskey was, for most Americans at least, a once-a-year drink.

Then Irish whiskey reinvented itself. Pioneering research in wood management made a difference in the flavor and quality of the whiskey. Distillery managers and blenders tracked barrels, sampling through their use and reuse, and set new parameters for first and second use. Marketing heads talked up using Irish whiskey in cocktails. The global rise in popularity of Irish-themed pubs helped as well.

The results have been an incredible stretch of growth for the category, albeit largely driven by sales of Jameson. But Jameson's rising tide has lifted the entire fleet of Irish whiskey boats. Tullamore Dew built a big new distillery, after having bought whiskey for decades.

The Teelings, father and son, have each built a new distillery; Beam Suntory has revived the old Kilbeggan distillery property; and a couple dozen all-new distilleries and companies have opened across the Republic. Bushmills, over the border in Northern Ireland, has been showing signs of an eagerness to regain its place in the forefront after a slow period. Scotch whisky giant Diageo has reentered the Irish category with a new brand, Roe & Co.

Redbreast 12 Year Old

Made with a significant portion of raw barley. Fresh-cut oak and sugared fresh fruit: melon, pear, apple. Beautiful fruit on the palate, floating on smooth, slippery malt. Gentle lingering finish.

What is the commonality of the whiskey they're all making? What is the identity of Irish whiskey? Once again, because of the variety of spirits, we're faced with "whiskey that's made in Ireland" as the only obvious answer. Once again, that won't do. We'll start with the regulated definitions.

The legal definition of Irish whiskey is set by the Republic and, by agreement, also applies to whiskey made in Northern Ireland. The latest iteration, known generally as "the Technical File," was set in 2014 and is generally parallel to the definition of Scotch whisky, with a few exceptions, one being the obvious one that the whiskey must be distilled and matured on the island of Ireland. Other "natural enzymes" are allowed to be added, and the whiskey is to be aged in "wooden casks, **such as oak**, not exceeding 700 litres [184.9 gallons] capacity." [emphasis added] That's a neat little loophole for not using oak barrels. Some distillers are taking advantage of that. Bushmills has an acacia wood–finished whiskey, and Midleton has done a chestnut finish.

The Technical File also lays out the three types of Irish whiskey. Malt Irish whiskey and grain Irish whiskey are very similar to their Scotch whisky counterparts, but the third, pot still Irish whiskey, is the unique contribution of Irish distillers to the class, mashed from a blend of malt, unmalted "raw" barley, and other grain/grains. It was called "pure pot still" in the market until 2011, when it was decided that "single pot still Irish" would be the new designation, which was accepted by the U.S. regulations and is still generally used on labeling. I'll refer to it as "single pot still" to avoid confusion.

Single pot still is at the heart of the big Irish blends. Blended Irish whiskey, like blended Scotch, is the biggest part of Irish whiskey production. Single pot still and Irish malt whiskeys give those blends the majority of their flavor.

But single pot still stands very well on its own—a fresh, vibrant whiskey with exceptional fruit notes. Irish Distillers and their legacy brands kept the type alive through the lean times: Redbreast and Green Spot, a whiskey that was "brokered," bottled from barrels of single pot still selected by Dublin wine merchants Mitchell & Son and sold at their shop. Mitchell & Son have since entered in a more formal joint venture with Irish Distillers (a subsidiary company of French drinks giant Pernod Ricard), and Green Spot is more widely available. It has also been joined by Yellow and Red, two other "Spot" whiskeys that had been retired. Irish Distillers has been very active in bottling other single pot still expressions such as Powers John's Lane and Barry Crockett Legacy.

Other distillers are making single pot still whiskey, though the definition in the Technical File has tripped up at least one. Kilbeggan recently released a "small batch rye," a whiskey that had both malted and raw barley included but also 30 percent rye.

The Technical File limits "other cereals" to a maximum of 5 percent of the total, which left Kilbeggan unable to use "single pot still" in their labeling for this whiskey. Some distillers are protesting the 5 percent limit, pointing to historical evidence that the amount of "other cereals" was often quite a bit higher.

Whiskey definitions do change. But the character of a national whiskey—like Irish, like Scotch, like bourbon—changes much more slowly. The character of Irish doesn't come from the commonly noted identifiers of the category, because every one of them has exceptions. Triple distilled? Not all of them. Unpeated? There are a few exceptions. Uses unmalted barley? Certainly not the Irish single malts; and they're not blended either—another identifier you might hear.

Irish whiskey is very much about Ireland. I talked to David Quinn, Irish Distillers' head of whiskey science and a longtime veteran of Irish distilling, about what made Irish whiskey Irish. After I poked holes in the usual identifiers just noted, he paused and thought. Perhaps, he mused, it's more about a gentleness, from a less hard-driving distillation in large pot stills that preserves more of the aromas from fermentation, from aging in a mild and consistent climate, from a blending philosophy that aims for a whiskey that is approachable and even friendly.

I think that's it. There are only a small number of Irish whiskeys that I'd classify as big, assertive, or menacing, while I have no problem finding plenty of Scotch whiskies or bourbons that fit those descriptors. That's the likely reason for Irish whiskey's meteoric growth over the past thirty years. It's making friends all over the world.

 Jameson

The best-selling Irish whiskey, a blend of grain whiskey and single pot still. Fresh apple and caramel, the Jameson signature. A bit of oak on the palate, some peppery notes, and more apple and caramel. Soothing, approachable.

Canadian

After the identity crises represented by defining Scotch and Irish whiskeys, Canadian whisky looks refreshingly simple.

Although every Canadian distiller does things a bit differently—sometimes more than "a bit"—there is a commendable commonality to their philosophy. While there are some exceptions to the rule, which we'll discuss, Canadian whisky is by and large blended whisky.

That's not so uncommon, of course. The huge majority of Scotch whisky is blended (yes, even now), and the dominant Irish and Japanese brands are blended. It's just that the Canadians do it their own way.

Blending in Canada follows the typical pattern of Scotch blends: An aged whisky distilled in a pot still is blended with an aged whisky distilled to a significantly higher proof in a column still. But whereas the traditional approach of the Scottish distillers to the use of more than one type of grain in their high-proof grain whisky is a mixed mashbill, cooking the grains together and aging the resulting distillate, Canadian distillers choose to make their single-grain "blending whiskies" in columns, age them separately, and then blend the resulting aged whiskies with the pot still "flavoring whiskies."

Canadian distillers recognize that this gives them many more options, more "distillate streams," as they describe them. You could age your corn whisky a bare three years in an ex-bourbon barrel, then put a wheat whisky in that used bourbon barrel and age it eight years. You can age a rye whisky in a cask that held sherry and blend it with corn whisky that had been aged in ex-bourbon barrels.

But Canadian distillers have an additional option. Canadian whisky regulations allow the inclusion of up to 9.09 percent other alcoholic beverages. So if a Canadian blender wants to accentuate the sherry character in a whisky beyond that imparted by aging the whisky in sherry barrels, then a small amount of actual sherry can be added.

You may already know this, but if that blew your mind, pause a second and consider what you thought. The knee-jerk reaction of the whisky aficionado to this is usually either a shout of "Blasphemy!" or a cynical assumption that this is being done to cut costs.

Let's look at the second judgment. Like many things involved in making whiskey, this can go either way. Bulk sherry is a cheap commodity right now due to a fall in popularity combined with an urgent need for seasoned sherry casks by whiskey makers. It would be easy to skimp on expensive sherry cask aging by simply blending in some cheap, flavorful sherry to gain a fruity overtone that could be varied to a desired effect. Some almost certainly do things like that, given that there are significant tax advantages if they add an American blending agent and then sell the resulting whisky in the United States.

But there are also Canadian whiskies that add small amounts of very expensive, high-quality sherries to achieve a fruity top note that no other whisky maker can achieve using traditional methods. Dr. Don Livermore, the blender for Corby, where he works on J. P. Wiser's, Lot No. 40, and Pike Creek, among others, has told me that the accountants shudder when they hear he's creating a new high-end whisky because they know that chances are good that he'll want to add something delicious—and expensive.

Now let's have a look at that other common reaction: "Blasphemy!" I'd argue that this reaction simply means that a person doesn't understand Canadian whisky. Those are the regulations. Those are the traditions. It's not blasphemy; it's holy writ!

I remember the moment when I started to get that, to really understand it. I was at Alberta Distillers, in Calgary, tasting some of their Alberta Premium line, including a masterful 25 year old. Tell me something, I asked Rick Murphy, the master distiller (since retired). American companies like WhistlePig are buying aged flavoring whisky in Canada and selling it for more than you charged for this fantastic whisky. Why not take that flavoring whisky you have in stock, create a new brand, and sell it yourselves? I thought it was a pretty smart idea.

Murphy didn't. "That's not how we make whisky," he told me, with a patient look on his face that I still remember. "You develop a blender's mind-set. It's a unique landscape."

If you're going to understand Canadian whisky, if you're going to add its unique and considerable pleasures to your regular whisky rotation, you're going to have to wrap your mind around that. To reject it is to reject Scotch whisky because it isn't aged in new, charred oak barrels. It is rejecting single pot still Irish whiskey because it uses raw barley instead of malt. It is rejecting bourbon because it uses the most common and cheap grain in the world as its base.

Exceptions to the Canadian Rule

Not every Canadian whisky follows the blending paradigm. Glenora, in Nova Scotia, makes malt whisky in copper pot stills.

Their Glen Breton malt whisky makes it plain that this is not Scotch, not made in Scotland. It is Canadian whisky because it's made in Canada and follows the fairly minimal requirements for that: mashed from cereal grains, aged in wood barrels for at least three years, and bottled at a minimum of 40% ABV.

There are also a number of new, small Canadian distillers who are essentially following their muses within those wide-open rules. They really play more in the craft whisky realm.

Instead, open your mind and try Canadian for what it is, for its possibilities. "It is the most innovative and adaptable whisky in the world," said Livermore. "The rules don't tell me how to use a mashbill, how to distill it, the type of barrel to use. It leaves the creativity to the blender. I wouldn't want to be a blender anywhere else."

It is somewhat refreshing to hear an unapologetic Canadian, isn't it? It's blended and proud.

Crown Royal

The best-selling Canadian whisky, blended the Seagram way. Caramel, toffee, and rich vanilla nose. Dark vanilla and toffee on the tongue, with hints of oak and cedar. Surprisingly long and warm finish.

American Bourbon and Rye

American rye whiskey is older than bourbon. Rye came here with European settlers and was being made well before the Revolutionary War.

That would have been an unaged spirit, probably flavored with spices or fruit.

I grew up in Pennsylvania Dutch country, where this kind of "whiskey" would have been common; and that tradition lived on in "cherry bounce," a concoction that was kept under the bar in a couple country inns I used to frequent. A jar of cherries, a scoop of brown sugar, topped up with rye whiskey. The bartender would pour shots off the top on occasion for regulars. A rye-soaked cherry was a special reward for a particularly witty story or difficult task performed.

Rye was a well-liked grain for whiskey partly because it grew well in marginal soil (and so vigorously that it would choke out most weeds). The other part is because its spicy, somewhat bitter flavor makes very tasty whiskey, even in relatively small additions, even before aging (and rye tastes good with a relatively short amount of aging, too). It's hard to argue with rye whiskey as a choice when no

less an American than George Washington decided to make it in retirement at Mount Vernon.

Rye moved west with the settlers who set up in the Monongahela River Valley in southwestern Pennsylvania. Settlers grew it in the rocky soil, harvested it, and in time-honored tradition, mashed and distilled it for easier transport. This Monongahela Rye, the first geographically famous whiskey from the young country, would be almost entirely rye or malted rye. Barley malt had more enzymatic power for converting starches to sugars, but it was not common on the frontier.

Neither was money, which led to trouble when the new nation decided to impose a tax on spirits. The Whiskey Rebellion was the result, and although it ended relatively peacefully, some of the more dissatisfied farmers decided to raft down the Ohio to join some folks in Kentucky who were making a new whiskey with a new grain from the New World: corn.

Let's set one thing straight, right now. No one is sure where the name "bourbon" comes from or exactly who decided to age it in charred oak barrels or even who decided to make it from corn. I won't go into the speculation here. We're talking about what it tastes like and why, and that is a result of a number of things that all came together over the course of about fifty years in Kentucky and Virginia and New Orleans.

Farmers found the rich bottomland soil produced fulsome crops of maize (American corn) and quickly figured out how to mash and distill it (because that's what farmers did back then). A scoop or two of rye or wheat made the whiskey more interesting than the straight-up sweetness of all-corn liquor. Finally, aging in a barrel with ¼ inch (0.6 cm) or so of char took away some of the roughness in exchange for pleasing notes of vanilla and caramel and gave the whiskey a nice reddish color. By the 1840s, everything was in place and we had a whiskey.

Unfortunately by the 1880s, we had screwed it up. Blenders calling themselves "rectifiers" were starting with cheap whiskey and adding flavoring and sugars to it using various recipes and labeling the result as "old bourbon." Bourbon distillers were horrified and realized that action had to be taken to protect their product's integrity. A group of distillers petitioned the government to regulate the industry.

The Wild Turkey Distillery, near Lawrenceburg, KY, is perched high above the Kentucky River.

The initial result was the Bottled in Bond Act of 1897, which set up a definition for "bottled in bond" spirits; bourbon would be chief among them. To be labeled as bottled in bond, a bourbon had to be the product of one distillery, all distilled in one six-month distilling "season," under the supervision of the same master distiller, and aged in a bonded warehouse under the scrutiny of a U.S. Treasury agent. Additionally it had to be at least four years old and bottled at 50 percent (100° proof). This represented a government (and industry) guarantee that the bourbon was pure, unadulterated, and sufficiently aged.

Some distillers found this too restrictive and asked for further regulation. The initial result was the Pure Food and Drug Act of 1906, but it was a compromise that no one was really happy with. In 1909, President Taft undertook to create a regulatory definition of whiskey. The Taft Decision, issued on December 27, 1909, is the core of what would become the "standards of identity," the current definition of American whiskey.

Briefly, Taft said that

- Whiskey had to be made from grain.

- A product that was all aged grain spirits was to be labeled "Straight Whiskey."

- If high-proof unaged grain distillate ("neutral spirits") was flavored with a percentage of whiskey, it had to be labeled as "Blended."

A critical addition would be made in 1938 when the requirement for new, charred oak containers for aging would be added, and—amazingly—the requirement that American whiskey be *made in America* was added only in 1964.

Compare these to the modern requirements, the standards of identity as they are put forth in the Code of Federal Regulations, Title 27, Subpart C, Section 5.22. (Amusingly this defining *American* regulation spells "whisky" without an "e" throughout. A change to the regulation has recently been proposed to acknowledge that

either spelling is acceptable.) There American "whisky"—bourbon, rye, and the others—is defined as being

- Distilled from a fermented grain mash of at least 51 percent corn in the case of bourbon (or rye, wheat, etc. for those respective whiskey types)

- Distilled to a proof no higher than 160° (80 percent ABV)

- Aged at a starting strength no higher than 125° proof, in a charred, new oak "container" (though no minimum period is given for the aging)

- Bottled at no less than 80° proof, with no coloring or flavoring added

- Further if it is aged for more than two years in the oak, it is "straight whiskey"; if it is aged fewer than four years, it must have an age statement on the label.

I believe that these regulations have a more direct impact on the flavor and character of bourbon and rye than do the other national whiskey regulations. The charred, new oak barrels are generally considered to be the source of at least 50 percent of the aroma and flavor of bourbon; some industry people believe it to be closer to 80 percent. No coloring and no flavoring means just that: none (although there is a small loophole that allows such materials in rye whiskey, though not if the whiskey is labeled as a "straight whiskey," so *caveat emptor*).

Corn and Used Barrels

Corn whiskey is a bit of an oddity in American whiskeys.

It is very focused in its makeup, required to have at least 80 percent corn in its mashbill. Corn whiskey has to be aged in used oak barrels or uncharred new oak barrels; it is not allowed to come in contact with charred wood. This, I assume, is a tribute to corn whiskey's early origins, prior to the common use of charred barrels. It results in a whiskey that is rich in corn flavor, with very little wood influence. Bourbon, naked, if you will. I'd suggest you try some corn whiskey if you haven't. Like the unaged new make spirits that

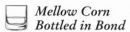

Mellow Corn
Bottled in Bond

Corn whiskey isn't bourbon. Try Mellow Corn, and you'll get corn—stewed, ground, baked—and some spicy notes of pepper. But there's no real oak character in this whiskey.

have become available for purchase in the past ten years or so, corn whiskey is a chance to taste whiskey the way it tasted at the dawn of the industrial age, some 200 years ago.

This also means that there is a large amount of overlap in the flavor profiles of the different American straight whiskeys. The new charred barrel and the prohibition of additives mean that the main differences among these whiskeys stem directly from the base grains, and those are some relatively subtle differences.

I compared the regulations governing Scotch whisky to the rules of chess, allowing almost infinite variety. Perhaps American whiskey's regulations are more similar to the rules of checkers (called "draughts" in the United Kingdom), a game popular in rural America. They are more direct, allowing fewer variables. But like checkers, these rules still allow a distiller to try new strategies, new moves, or even renewed ones from games long past, in a never-ending round of enjoyment—for the consumer.

Very Old Barton
Bottled in Bond

A bourbon that's maybe not as familiar as some. Nose rips with heat, clove, and oak; sharp edged. Not a soft sweet bourbon; this is spicy, hot, more lean and mean. Stand-up stuff; an exhilarating ride.

Japanese

Japan is the youngest whisky region. Their whisky industry is about to celebrate its first full century. The first commercial distillation of whisky in Japan was in December 1924.

The distiller (and distillery engineer) was a legendary figure in Japanese whisky, Masataka Taketsuru. He studied chemistry at the University of Glasgow and apprenticed at several Scotch distilleries. He returned home, where he went to work for the Kotobukiya company (which would become Suntory), and helped establish the Yamazaki distillery. He left Suntory in the early 1930s and started his own company, Nikka, on the northern island of Hokkaido. These two companies still dominate Japanese whisky, though there are some much smaller distillers.

As you might guess from the path of Taketsuru, Japanese whisky is much like Scotch whisky. It is mainly single malt and grain whiskies, and the biggest sellers are blended whiskies. They largely buy their peated malt from Scotland and age their whisky in used bourbon and sherry barrels. But they also use some barrels made of Japanese oak, *mizunara*. Mizunara is expensive and somewhat rare, and it requires longer aging of the spirit—fifteen to twenty years—to reach balance.

That's one difference, and there are others that are more subtle. The Japanese whisky makers filter their distiller's beer, the wash, through a lauter tun for a clear wash. Not all Scotch distillers use a cloudy wash, but many do, and the difference is in a nutty, cereal note that the cloudy wash will create. The clear wash gives a cleaner, more neutral palate that allows other flavors to come through. The Japanese distillers also use multiple yeast strains (and beneficial bacteria; remember the Scotch whisky regulations edict on that?), while the Scotch distillers will have one house yeast that they use for every fermentation.

That leads to another major difference: in-house production of multiple whiskies. This may not sound like a big deal, but it is. Scotch whisky distillers have a network of agreements, referred to as "reciprocity," whereby they trade whisky with each other to create the blends they sell. Japanese distillers not only don't have that many distilleries to trade among, but they do not have such an arrangement and never have—probably going back to the rocky initial relationship between Nikka and Suntory.

As a result, Japanese distillers have built the ability to create different flavors within their own facilities. They have multiple yeast strains, they have different types of stills, they will run malt whisky through a column still, and there are a variety of barrels used, including the mizunara oak, ex-bourbon and ex-sherry, and in at least one whisky, the Hibiki blend made by Suntory—barrels that held plum liqueur. The ability to create and innovate inevitably leads to the impulse to create and innovate.

I've found Japanese whiskies in general to be well integrated, not overbearing or unbalanced. To say they reflect a value in Japanese culture for "oneness" might be too facile—or it might be right on the nose. The student may not be

said to have surpassed the master—Scotch whisky yields nothing on quality—but the student is certainly no longer a student.

Japanese whisky is fully mature, individual, and distinct. The only thing it needs to achieve now is greater supply. As the world market has discovered Japanese whisky over the past fifteen years or so, we have grabbed as much as we could, a testimonial to its quality. Now the distillers just need time to make more.

🥃 Hibiki Harmony

Blended whisky that brings elegance to the glass. Malt, light oak, sandalwood, and a hint of fruit on the nose. Malt sweetness soothes, and the nose comes true on the tongue in a gentle whole. Unity.

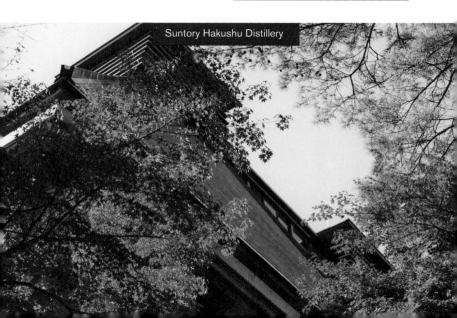

Suntory Hakushu Distillery

Craft

I don't like the term "craft whiskey" any more than I like the term "craft distiller."

It's imprecise and unclear in its meaning. It reflects poorly on the legacy distillers, who, most new distillers will grant, make excellent and interesting whiskey.

We inherited the term from parallels to "craft brewer," from a market of similar small upstarts that has been hugely successful. But that category is now in the process of walking away from the term (in favor of "independent brewer," apparently) because it is imprecise and doesn't adapt well to success. If a craft brewer is, essentially, a small new brewer, what does it become when it is successful and twenty years old?

That's why I tell new distillers any time the subject comes up, don't use the term "craft." It's going to be problematic. And I'm going to start using another term—just as soon as somebody comes up with one. Until then, I guess I'll have to bow to the commonality and say "craft distiller."

Who are the craft distillers? I'm not just talking about the new distillers in America. ("New" is somewhat relative, anyway, since some of them have been making whiskey for almost twenty years.)

These are the new distillers in the five whiskey regions, plus the ones everywhere else. There are more than thirty in Tasmania, for instance, and more than forty in France.

These are small distillers with big ideas. They are people who want to make whiskey in their home country, in their hometown. They may want to make whiskey very similar to something they had that made an impression.

Steve McCarthy, who makes fruit brandies and eaux-de-vie at his Clear Creek Distillery in Portland, Oregon, tells the story of how he found himself on vacation in Scotland, trapped in his hotel by days of lashing rain, with only a pool table and a supply of Lagavulin for diversion. Inspired by the whisky, he came up with McCarthy's Oregon Single Malt, made from Scottish peated malt but aged in Oregon oak barrels.

Craft distillers often use heirloom or hybrid grains, sometimes from very local farmers, sometimes grain they grow themselves. They use nontraditional grains, like triticale, spelt, or quinoa (not technically a grain, but the federal government is considering a change to the standards of identity that will allow it). They use hybrid stills, stills of their own design; and at least one distiller, Leopold Brothers in Denver, uses a three-chamber still, an archaic design once popular among the Pennsylvania and Maryland rye whiskey distillers, the first one made in almost 100 years.

Craft distillers sometimes make bourbon without the sour mash technique; ten years ago, I could write that every bourbon distiller used sour mash without fear of contradiction. They use a variety of wood, they may bathe the barrels with music as they age, there are distillers who put their barrels to age in shipping containers, and there are distillers who put their barrels *on ships* to age.

American Single Malt

Only in America is a used barrel considered to be abnormal.

The staple of Scotch, Irish, Japanese, and Canadian whiskey making, the used barrel in America was employed only in a few brands of corn whiskey and Brown-Forman's Early Times "Kentucky whisky."

By the standards of identity, the most popular types of whiskey—bourbon, rye, wheat—have to be aged in new, charred oak containers. Used barrels are only allowed in a few types, and there is no category for "American single malt whiskey."

So when American craft distillers wanted to make an American spin on malt whiskey, they were faced with a hard decision. Use new, charred barrels, or age in used barrels and be forced to call the product some sort of relatively

unappealing name, like "whiskey distilled from malt mash," or merely "whiskey."

Some distillers are pressing the government regulators to create a new "American single malt" category, with 100 percent malt and used barrels as a key component. Until such time, distillers are aging malt whiskey in new barrels and aging "whiskey" made of 100 percent malt in used barrels.

Westward

is American malt whiskey. Clean, sweet cereal malt nose with furniture oak (dry and rough carved); spices and fruit roll across the tongue on a bed of malt. Great spicy-sweet finish with an intriguing hint of anise.

AMERICAN SINGLE MALT

Darek Bell, the cofounder of Corsair Distillery in Nashville, told me once about operating in "the shadow of Jack Daniel's," as he put it. Craft distillers have to realize that they're not going to be able to make a business on making whiskey just like Jack Daniel's, he said. Packaging costs money, marketing costs money, advertising and promotion cost money.

"But," he said with a smile, "creativity is free." Craft distillers have to break traditions and traditional expectations in order to compete, in order to make their mark. They can drill deep on the local angle, like Cedar Ridge in Iowa, where they make much of their state's excellent quality corn crop. They can dig into history, like Leopold Bros. and their still, or Mountain Laurel Spirits, near Philadelphia, where they use a historical mashbill for Monongahela-style rye. They may hitch up with a brewer to make whiskey from dark beers, heavily hopped beers, wheat beers, and more.

Several distillers use only organic ingredients; others use exclusively non-GMO grains. (To be fair, so do Four Roses and a number of Scotch distillers.) Some do their own malting, sometimes smoking the malt with local peat or varied woods; one uses corncobs to smoke the corn for their whiskey.

That's the similarity of craft whiskey: difference. Craft whiskey is seeking to do something different. They do it for the challenge, they do it for fun, and they do it for profit, in the end, because difference is what sells these whiskeys. Craft distillers give us the chance to find out "what if." And that's often worth the price of admission to their wild, wonderful circus.

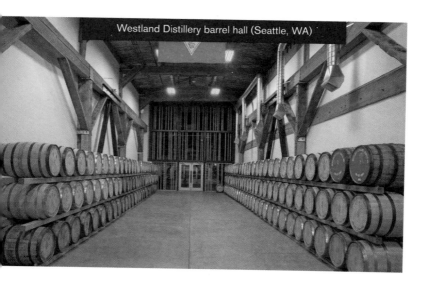

Westland Distillery barrel hall (Seattle, WA)

When Is a Craft Distillery Not a Craft Distillery?

Using the term "craft distillery" seems perfectly appropriate for small, new places, or even when we're talking about a place that's maybe ten years old, with twenty-five employees and an output of fewer than 20,000 cases a year.

But what about a place like Kavalan, in Taiwan, backed with the resources of the King Car Company and capable of producing more than 1 million cases a year? Or Mackmyra, in Sweden, with a capacity for more than 65,000 cases? Both are selling whiskey well in the export market.

There are ten new distilleries in America with a capacity that would put them in the top 20 (one, O. Z. Tyler, in the top 10) in the country, sizable and comfortably medium sized. There are others in the planning stages that are in that same range. Does size matter?

What do you call a distillery that is small but owned by a much larger distilling company that allows it to operate with a measure of independence?

These are all questions that craft brewing has had to answer, and generally the answers have been mixed, depending on who's asking and who's answering.

 Baby Blue

Bourbon made with Hopi blue corn. Nose is sweet, corn pudding, honey notes; some spice in a light, sweet rush on the tongue; cocoa notes as it fades. A small distiller favorite of mine.

The Grain

Chapter 3:

There are legal definitions of whiskey in several countries, none exactly the same. There are the definitions of various distillers' associations, which are understandably self-referential (and often self-serving). There are cultural ones, which often overlap with the legal and business definitions. Then there are personal ones, what whiskey means to each of us, the drinkers.

Despite the regional differences in those definitions, in barrels and stills and aging, they all have one basic thing in common. All whiskey is made from grain, from cereals. Not fruit, vegetables, honey, cane, or milk (really, milk); those are sources for other spirits. But if you're going to call what you make or sell or drink "whiskey," it has to be distilled from fermented grain. (There are spirits made largely from sugarcane in Asia that are called "whiskey," but only in their native countries. The rest of the world doesn't consider them to be whiskey.)

This is an odd thought at first. Grain is dry, not like fruits or honey or pressed sugarcane. Even when you cut it open, what you find are hard, insoluble starches, bound in a matrix of proteins, none of which will ferment. But that grain also has a sprout, with a chemical trigger that can convert those starches to sugars; and that's what we want for whiskey. Of the four major grains used to make whiskey—barley, corn, rye, and wheat—barley is the one with the quickest pull on that trigger, the one that's easiest to convert. We'll start with it because that eagerness to convert makes it the key to making all types of whiskey.

Barley & Malt

Barley (Hordeum vulgare) *has been a partner of humankind for at least 12,000 years, one of our earliest cultivated crops.*

The history and mythology of the Fertile Crescent, the rich Middle Eastern area that was the origin of human civilization, is bound to barley cultivation. Barley was made into bread, and it was soon learned that if the barley was allowed to germinate, to sprout, those hard starches turned into soluble starches. We call that process malting, and it's a vital step on the way to turning starches to sugars, which leads directly to fermentation, beer, and finally whiskey.

Barley grows in a range of climates, though it's not as well adapted to truly cold climates as is rye. There are two major types of domesticated barley: two-row and six-row, named for the number of kernel rows on the ears. Most barley is grown for animal feed, with only the exceptional barley going to brewers and distillers.

The six-row strains tend to grow better in North America, and they have a higher diastatic power, a greater ability to convert starch to sugar. That's very important, as we'll soon learn. The two-row barley strains grow better in

Europe and are favored for Scotch and Irish whiskeys. Agronomists are constantly creating new barley cultivars with improved traits for feed and beverage use. Distillers are generally looking for the highest yield of spirit per unit of grain.

Barley is a grain that almost seems designed to be fermented. Barley's low gluten content doesn't make for great bread, but it has a substantial husk that makes a natural filter bed during mashing, holding back the spent bits of grain while the dissolved sugars run away with the water.

But most importantly, barley malts easily and consistently. While many grains can be malted, barley is by far the favorite, so much so that while other malted grains are named specifically—"malted wheat," "malted rye"—malted barley is known simply as malt. Best of all, malting barley yields a rich surplus of the enzymes needed for starch conversion; that's the diastatic power mentioned above. The surplus is so large that other nonmalted grains can be ground

up with it and the whole mixture will convert. That's the reason you'll find about 15 percent malt in most bourbon mashbills.

Here's how malting works: When grains sprout, enzymes are released that convert the hard, insoluble starches in the barleycorn into softer, soluble starches that are ready to be used for food for the new plant. But we don't want plants—we want whiskey and beer—so we trick the grain into thinking it's time to sprout. This takes about two days and enough water to soak the grains.

You can feel the difference in the hardness of the grain as it converts. When I was visiting Bowmore Distillery, on Islay, I was shown an old-school method for checking the progress, called "chalking the malt." Workers would take a grain and rub it against a dark plaster or stone wall. If the grain left a white mark, the starches were almost completely converted, and it was about ready.

When the malt maker (the maltster) judges that conversion is complete, the malt is heated in a kiln. It's a balance: You want to kill the sprout and drive off most of the water; but if it gets too hot, the malt will roast or, worse, those crucial enzymes will break down. Successful kilning leaves the grain, now called "malt," in a condition to be bagged, shipped, and stored until it's time to grind it for processing.

Barley was seemingly made to be fermente
Shown here being raked, resting patiently
and sprouting

From Malt to Whiskey

Single malt and blended malt Scotch whiskies are made from all malt, as are single malt Japanese whiskies and the many new American single malt whiskeys. It may be partly or all smoked malt, depending on the distiller and the planned whiskey.

American whiskeys like bourbon and rye usually have between 10 percent and 15 percent malt, primarily used for an enzymatic boost rather than flavor, though there is a small contribution to the flavor from the malt. Canadian whisky makers tend to add enzymes directly, rather than by using malt. Small distillers may use the more traditional malt addition, or they may add enzymes, depending on circumstances.

Irish whiskey is more varied, and some, like Bushmills, may be all malt. The single pot still uses a mixture of malted barley and unmodified, "raw" barley in the mash, which gives a fresh grassy and fruity character to the whiskey, along with a certain oiliness. The practice became widespread in Ireland after the imposition of a tax on malt in 1785, but it appears to have been used before, presumably for reasons of flavor rather than costs.

One thing that's been baffling to me, as someone who has been enjoying and writing about beer longer than I have about whiskey, is the tiny number of whiskeys that take advantage of the wide array of malts that brewers use regularly. The malt distillers use is what brewers call "pale malt," the most common type and the simplest. But brewers use malts that are roasted black, toasted brown, "stewed" to crystallize; there are more than 100 different types of malt. But most whiskey makers use only one or two. The craft distillers are turning this around.

When you're making whiskey, you may use malt for the sweet, somewhat delicate flavor (and you may use unmodified barley for that Irish freshness). But malt's powerful enzymes ensure it a place in most distilleries.

Peat & Malt

I like telling people that single malt whisky is about as simple as it gets. It only has two ingredients, after all: water and malt. (There's yeast, but it comes out before distillation. Is that an outgredient?). That's knowingly overlooking one of the most defining flavors of Scotch whisky: the smoky presence or clean absence of peat. That flavor enters Scotch by smoking the malt over a peat fire, so let's have a look at that.

Peat is decayed vegetation—like moss, leaves, grass, flowers— that accumulates over centuries in bogs and ponds. The water that's held in place by the moss keeps oxygen away from the plant matter, so it doesn't rot. More and more plants die and fall into the water, and the mass presses down. Given hundreds of millions of years and a lot more weight, it would become coal. But in about 1,000 years, it becomes peat.

Like coal, peat can be burned once it's dug out of the bog and dried. It is a smoky and aromatic fire. When my wife and I were on our honeymoon in Ireland in 1989, a lot of homes and pubs still burned peat fires; and the air was hazy and the reek was thick.

That smoke is the same smoke you'll find in whiskies like Ardbeg, Talisker, and Highland Park. When the malt is still wet, just after the final turning, it's put in the kiln and a smolder of peat is built beneath the slotted floor.

The smoking goes on for up to twenty hours, after which the peat won't absorb much more smoke. I've stood in the kiln at this point; it's humid but not terribly hot, or even that smoky. The wet malt is absorbing the smoke, binding it to the husks.

The smokiness of the malt is measured in parts per million (ppm) of phenols, the aromatic compounds in the smoke. It's as much as 70 ppm in strongly peated malts. The phenols in malt versus the phenols in the actual spirit are at about a 3:1 ratio. Much of the smoke is locked in the husks and left behind in the mashing process. You're better off staying subjective. Drink the whisky and see how smoky it tastes to you.

Whiskies differ in how much peat smoke they put to the malt, but they also vary from using different peats. There are regional differences related to rainfall and temperature, but every bog has different plants growing in it.

Some peats are therefore more floral, some more grassy, some more acrid, some more savory. It is now believed by some researchers that the "seaside" or "briny" character of some whiskies comes from the peat used in malting. (That's still somewhat subjective, and much is still open to debate.)

One thing does need to be reinforced: Whisky doesn't get a peaty aroma or flavor from using water that has run through a peat bog. As retired Bowmore master distiller Eddie MacAffer told me, "Just a romantic notion." Peat pretty much smells like dirt; you only get that distinctive smoky smell by burning it.

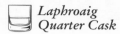

Laphroaig Quarter Cask

Big peat, little cask. Like a bonfire and some deeply smoked smelt. Wood smoke and sweet malt on the palate, rolling all over themselves. Never-ending smoky finish.

PEAT & MALT

Cut peat shown draining in the grass

Other Grains

Malt and corn are the most common grains used in making whiskey. Rye and wheat run a distant third and fourth, but they are still far more common than any other grains distillers may use to make whiskey. There are whiskeys being made with oats, blue corn, and hybrid grains like triticale, a wheat/rye cross. Millet and teff are also used, often in small proportions, sometimes as the dominant grain.

Different strains of the common grains are also used, like the Bloody Butcher and Wapsie Valley corn varieties or Golden Promise barley, most of them "heritage" strains that may not be as productive as today's standards but offer interesting differences in flavors. There are also early varieties, almost fossils in their age, from the dawn of cultivation. There are early strains of wheat that can be used: emmer wheat, club wheat, spelt, freekeh, bulgur, all of them offering something different (both to distillers and the farmers who supply them).

Then there are the so-called pseudocereals: quinoa, amaranth, and buckwheat, all of which are technically seeds, not grains.

They have been used to make spirits that have been aged like whiskey, and called "whiskey" by some producers. At the time I'm writing this, there is a proposed change to American federal regulations that would allow spirits made from these cereals to be labeled as "whiskey." Having tasted quinoa and buckwheat whiskeys, I welcome that addition; they make interesting spirits!

🥃 Catskill Distilling The One and Only Buckwheat

80 percent buckwheat. Earthy aromas of hickory nuts and autumn leaves, a bit of cinnamon. Creamy mouthfeel, more nuts, sweet oaken vanilla, and more dry leaves at the end. Unique, compelling.

Corn

Corn is a hugely important grain in whiskey production, second only to barley.

It is the primary grain in America's largest-selling whiskey, bourbon; but it might surprise you to learn that the Canadian whisky makers, on the whole, use more corn than any other grain as well. Corn's a pretty surprising grain overall.

Zea mays is a giant grass that has its origins in the Americas. It is a heavily modified grain, believed to be bred from a beneficial mutation of a wild grass called teosinte, which can still be found in rural Central America. It's worth noting this because humans have worked with this grass and made it much more than it was. From a waving multistalked weed, corn has become the most important cereal crop in the world, grown on every populated continent and producing a bigger annual harvest than any other grain, including wheat and rice.

About 40 percent of that crop grows in the United States. Americans took corn from a highly productive grain in the 1800s—when 9 pounds (4.1 kg) of seed per acre would yield a farmer about 1,100 pounds (499 kg) at harvest—to today's amazing example of hybrid vigor. American farmers will now plant 19 pounds (8.6 kg) of seed corn on an acre and expect to harvest 11,000 pounds (4989.5 kg)—five and a half tons!—of yellow dent corn in the fall. Research plots are delivering yields up to 20,000 pounds (9071.8 kg) per acre from less than 50 pounds (22.7 kg) of seed, proving corn is still evolving.

Fermenting bourbon mash

From Corn to Whiskey

Yellow dent corn is the type most used in the whiskey business. It arrives at distilleries in trucks and railcars, a yellow river of grain.

One of the easiest quality tests done on this incoming corn is to heat a random sample in a microwave. If the hot corn smells right, with no off aromas, the load is more than likely acceptable, though it is still tested for nitrogen and moisture content and visually checked for evidence of mold.

Corn is bursting with starches, but they're a different set of starches than in malt, rye, or wheat; so corn has to be milled and precooked before mashing. Some distillers cook the corn under pressure, and some just do a longer boil, though both gelatinize the starches, making the corn ready for the mash.

Corn also has a distinct, sweet flavor that stays with the liquid throughout the process, from mashing to fermenting to distilling. That flavor and abundant fuel for the creation of alcohol are what corn brings to the whiskey equation.

Rye

Rye has some strange habits. It grows almost as tall as corn, though it looks more like wheat and barley, with a classic grass-grain stalk and head.

It will grow almost anywhere it can get a toehold; I once saw rye growing in a 0.4-inch (1 cm)-deep skiff of dust on a tractor blade. Farmers call these unplanned plants "volunteers," and you can sometimes see them sticking up above the other plants in a field of wheat or barley. Rye also acts up in the distillery, where it is notorious for causing billowing foam during mashing.

Well, what can you expect from an adolescent? Rye (*Secale cereale*) only recently joined barley around the human fireplace. Archaeological evidence for rye in active cultivation goes back only about 3,500 years, making it a newcomer, which is probably why the Roman historian Pliny the Elder was so dismissive of it. He complained that this northern grain "is a very poor food and only serves to avert starvation" and that it had a "bitter taste— most unpleasant to the stomach."

Pliny got the bitterness part right. But that bitterness, what we now think of as spiciness, is part of what makes rye so attractive to whiskey makers and drinkers. Rye has a full fan of tastes: bitter, mint, grassiness, pepper, and more. It was probably shocking to Pliny's wheat-accustomed palate, but in a glass, it's wonderful.

The other thing that makes rye attractive to farmers is its hardiness, which Pliny also noted: "It will grow upon any soil, and yields a hundred-fold; it is employed also as a manure for enriching the land." Farmers say rye will grow on rock, and rye is a dominating grass, growing so quickly that it barely needs weeding. Those long stalks make for a good cover crop, returning plenty of sun-spawned nutrients to the soil when they're plowed under.

That's largely how rye has survived in the United States, as a cover crop to hold soil in place during fallow seasons between cash crops. Rye was a popular crop in Eastern Europe and Scandinavia because it could grow on rocky soil or in cold climates, and that's why you find rye bread there. When those folks emigrated to early America, they found that rye grew in the stony soil of western Pennsylvania; and that's what they grew and distilled. Canadian distillers took to rye for similar reasons—and for the great dose of flavor that even a small amount of rye can give to whiskey.

"Rye whiskey" means different things in different places; depending on the regulations, it may have a minimum of 51 percent rye in the mix or only a token amount. Some whiskeys are 100 percent rye, thanks to rye malt or added enzymes. But the reason it's in there, rye's ticket to the whiskey dance, is that punch of flavor it gives a spirit.

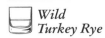 *Wild Turkey Rye*

Traditional Kentucky-type rye. Spicy and sweet, like red hots or old-fashioned hard candy. Corn is sweet on the tongue; rye is somewhat bitter. A real push-pull. Screaming for a cocktail.

Wheat

*Common wheat (*Triticum aestivum*) has been with humans almost as long as barley. It, too, was grown in the Fertile Crescent but overtook and surpassed barley in value and importance.*

We eat wheat, while most barley is fed to animals. Wheat is second only to corn in volume of production. When it comes to whiskey, wheat is an important second choice to rye in making bourbon and is slowly gaining acceptance as a primary grain in whiskey as well. Bourbon is required to be a minimum of 51 percent corn, and a certain amount of malt is needed for the enzymatic push to convert starches to sugars. The third grain in bourbon is most often rye, but a significant—and prized—number of bourbons use wheat instead, among them Maker's Mark, Old Fitzgerald, Rebel Yell, Weller, and Van Winkle.

Why do these bourbons use wheat? Some of the reason is that it simply isn't rye. "Wheaters" don't have that rye bite but instead deliver a softer palate, one where the corn has more of a chance to shine through. Wheated bourbons also have a light aroma of whole wheat bread and may taste sweeter than a high-rye bourbon. Wheat whiskeys, where wheat makes up more than 51 percent of the mashbill, bring an even softer palate.

I've found that they're a great introduction to the barrel-forward flavors of American whiskeys.

You'll find a variety of opinions on what wheat adds—or doesn't add—to a whiskey, even among master distillers; but the strong sales of these whiskeys prove that whatever it is, it's popular. Call it softness, call it smoothness, or call it manners: That's what wheat brings to the table.

We have our cast of characters. Now it's time to put them in play, let them mingle, and get to work together. That's our next step in building whiskey flavor: mashing.

 Bernheim

A 7-year-old wheat whiskey, over 51 percent wheat. Bright, fresh nose of cinnamon and sassafras root with oak framing. Lean, warming on the palate, firm oak spice with a restrained sweet finish.

The Mash

Chapter 4

Ground grains,
or grist, falling
into the mash turn

When the grain arrives at the distillery, it's hard, dry, and about as far from the idea of a great-tasting glass of whiskey as we'll be in the entire process. The job is to somehow go from dry and dusty to wet and tasty.

To do that, you have to get at what's inside the grain, the starch that the plant has stored there to feed the seed when it sprouts. We've got to steal that, pulverize it, and wet it down so that we can turn it into sugar, pretty much against the seed's will. Once we have sugars, we can unleash the yeast; but we have to get at that starch first.

It's time to mill and mash. Milling is a fairly simple proposition: crushing the grain into a fine grist. Does the size of the grist affect the flavor? Dr. Pat Heist, cofounder of Wilderness Trail Distillery in Danville, Kentucky, compared it to coffee. "It's like a drip grind versus an espresso grind," he said. "You can get a slightly different flavor."

There are two types of mill in general use: the hammer mill and the roller mill. Roller mills are very easy to explain. You have two heavy metal rollers placed horizontally and very close to each other; the gap is adjustable. The rollers rotate in opposite directions, in such a way that both are turning in toward the top of the gap. Grain is fed into the gap area, and friction pulls it in, where the rollers crush it. There may be an additional set of rollers below to crush the grain more finely and consistently.

The hammer mill is a bit more complicated. There is a rapidly rotating frame inside a cage of steel that's pierced with a web of uniformly spaced and sized holes. On the surface of the frame are sets of freely rotating hammers, metal bars designed to slam into the grain as it drops around the outside of the frame. Very tight tolerances leave the hammers swinging just barely above the surface of the cage. The impact of the hammers smashes the grain against the holes in the cage, and the grains are broken and quickly pounded into flour.

Both mills develop similar grades of consistently sized flour from the four grains used in most distilling: corn, malt, wheat, and rye. Distillers have preferences, of course. Some feel that a hammer mill damages the grain and heats it too much. Others feel that a roller mill isn't as efficient as a hammer mill. It seems like they always like best what they already have, and that's probably a lot of it. There's no definitive scientific literature on the difference that either side could point to.

Too Good to Survive

"And you'll want to get a picture of our Porteus mill," the distillery manager mentioned as we entered the grain-handling area of one of the Islay distilleries. "I will?" I thought. "Why?"

The mill was an attractive shade of dark red, and the nameplate said "Porteus" in beautiful old-timey script. But surely a mill's a mill. Only it is more than that if it's a Porteus mill.

What's the big deal with the Porteus mill? For one thing, that particular one has been milling malt since about 1900. For another, the Porteus mills were so solidly built that they put the company out of business (the same thing happened to their only real competitor, the Boby company). They didn't break down and they couldn't really be improved upon, so when people stopped building distilleries, there were no sales of new mills. They're so well made that when new Scotch whisky distilleries start up these days, some of them try to find an old Porteus mill because they're simply the best.

The last I heard, that same mill is still chugging away. And now I do take a picture any time I see a Porteus mill.

Recipes

Single malt whiskies have a very simple recipe: malt. By regulation, a Scotch single malt whisky must be 100 percent barley malt. It may be a mix of malts—peated, unpeated, different strains—but all malt.

Other whiskeys labeled as "single malt" are under similar constraints, but within those constraints there are obviously ways to maneuver and find flavor. I'm always impressed by the number of Scotch malt whiskies that are made with peated malt from the Port Ellen maltings on Islay that manage to make a whisky with a distinctive and individual peat character. That's real skill.

American whiskey regulations, the standards of identity, treat "malt whisky" like bourbon, only made with malt instead of corn as the main grain. The mashbill has to be at least 51 percent malt, and other grains are allowed. There is no legal definition for "single malt whisky" in the standards. Sometimes, reading the standards really brings to mind the adage: "When all you have is a hammer, everything looks like a nail."

American whiskeys and Irish single pot still whiskeys are the ones most likely to have a mixed mashbill. Canadian distillers will make their whisky with different grains but often distill them separately, age them separately, and then blend.

Bourbon is made with a mashbill of anywhere from 51 percent up to 80 percent corn, then 10 percent to 15 percent malt, and the rest rye or wheat. The corn is there for sugar and flavor, the malt is there for enzymes for conversion, and the rye or wheat is for its own flavor, a twist of spice, or softness. The different mashbills may lean heavier on corn for sweetness or rye for spice, but there's not really a lot of flavor from the malt. It's there for the enzymes.

"That's the same whiskey."

Is a mashbill the same thing as a "recipe"?

I do hear a lot of people saying that so-and-so bourbon from Distillery A is "the same mashbill as this-and-that bourbon, which costs $30 less; it's the same bourbon, different label."

Sure it is, and this pancake is the same as this waffle, this funnel cake, or these crepes—except they're not. They're all made from flour, sugar, baking powder, eggs, milk, and butter; but they're prepared differently.

A mashbill isn't a recipe; it's just a list of ingredients. It doesn't matter if it's bourbon, rye, or single pot still Irish. Mix and mash them, and it may still be the same. But then you can use different yeasts, different fermentation times; you can use different stills or different still settings, different barrels, different warehouses or floors in the warehouses, and of course, you can leave them in the warehouse for different periods of time. Then the blender gets hold of them, and anything can happen.

Same mashbill, same whiskey? Don't you believe it. And if you're not convinced, just look at single malt whiskeys and their diverse range of flavors:

Scotch, Irish, Japanese, American, English, Indian, Taiwanese. All different, and all with *exactly* the same "mashbill," 100 percent malt. The other variables in the process make the difference. Case closed.

🥃 Basil Hayden vs. Old Grand-Dad Bonded

Same mashbill, yeast, barrel—different whiskeys. Basil: Oak and light cinnamon, oily rye on the tongue, quick finish. Grand-Dad: Vanilla, oak, bare hint of spice, explodes on tongue with sweet cinnamon and hammering oak. Hello, warehouse influence.

A peek inside the still

Time for Some Magic

We've milled our grains, and the grist is ready to go. Wait, we're almost ready: Are we mashing with corn?

We'll need to cook it beforehand to gelatinize corn's particularly well-integrated starches. It's not really a flavor-creation step—just a way to get the corn converted better.

Speaking of which, I don't want to raise any expectations. Mashing is a crucial step in distillation, but it is more of a preparatory step to flavor creation. I'll let Ian Palmer, the distilling wizard who's just starting up the new InchDairnie Distillery in Scotland, explain.

"Mashing is all about conversion, starch into sugar," he says. "Without that there would be very little fermentation. Mashing is about creating the circumstances allowing the creation of the basic flavors in the fermentation. So its impact on flavor is more indirect than direct."

With all the mash in the cooking vessel, the "mash tun," we have a green light for conversion.

Conversion is an enzymatic process. Naturally occurring enzymes in the malt are activated by water and the right temperature. The brewer "hydrates" the grist (now called the "mash") by mixing in hot water. It may be set at the temperature needed to bring the mash to the proper temperature for the enzymes to work, in which case no further heating is needed. Or the distiller may raise the temperature of the mash in steps to activate different enzymes at different stages to increase efficiency.

It's precise work. If the temperature of the mash is too low, the enzymes aren't activated; too high, and they'll break down before they get their work done. But when that conversion happens, the thick, starchy mash suddenly turns slippery, thin, and slick with sugar. It's a stunningly evident physical transformation.

I'll mention that some distillers add enzymes to the mash (the practice is not allowed in Scotland). The enzymes are grown up using molds, in a similar fashion to the use of koji in sake. They are usually kept and applied in liquid form.

Water's Small, Crucial Contribution

Water is essential to making whiskey, but it's not a huge factor in flavor creation. It's more like a factor that can only make whiskey flavors terrible, unless you get it right.

Iron in water can ruin whiskey. It will turn black and taste wretched. One of the most important things about a water source for making whiskey is that it be iron free. Kentucky's vaunted limestone water, Scotland's free-flowing springs, Ireland's mystic wells, Japan's forested streams, and Canada's plentiful lakes all provide iron-free water—as do the municipal water systems of nearby towns these days.

But it's not just iron. There's also *geosmin*, a word that sounded so odd when I first heard it that I assumed it was something folksy, made up. But it's real, an organic compound ($C_{12}H_{22}O$) formed by bacteria that's found in water and in soil. It is a made-up word, but made up by biologists who identified it in 1965 and named it from the Greek words *geo* ("earth") and *osme* ("odor"): earth smell.

Geosmin is responsible for the earthy smell of beets and the musty, earthy smell of some lake water. It's a key part of petrichor, another interesting word; that's the smell that comes after rain falls on dry, warm earth. It can also most definitely get into

whiskey, as people of a certain age can attest. I know I tasted it in my youth and thought it was part of the flavor of bourbon, which is why I became a Glenlivet drinker in grad school. That mustiness doesn't happen anymore. Distillers are aware of geosmin now and filter it out.

For more about water and what whiskey needs from it, I talked to Liz Rhoades, a senior research scientist in fermentation, distillation, and maturation for Diageo, based in Illinois. The first thing she brought up was mineral content.

"Limestone water has a higher content of calcium and magnesium," she noted. "Both of these minerals are key to yeast performance and also provide buffering capacity in the fermenting mash, keeping stress levels low. Therefore, an effect on flavor, typically in a positive way."

Ian Palmer noted that Scottish distillers relied on their spring water to make mashing and fermentation possible.

"Originally spring water was essential," he said, "as the barley itself did not have all of the trace elements present for all the process to work, conversion and fermentation in particular. Today there is less need for spring water, but it always helps. Zinc is a very good example: No zinc, no fermentation—it's that simple."

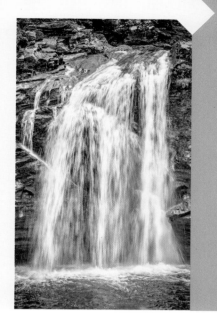

Most distillers simply buy them; a few culture them up themselves. Alberta Distillers, the rye whisky specialists in Calgary, not only do this but have bred their enzymes to work best on rye and to neutralize the foaming rye causes in fermentation.

Why add enzymes? Some do it to boost the enzymes from the malt, but some distillers will set a mashbill without any malt—or with only token amounts—and rely on the added enzymes alone for conversion. Liz Rhoades notes that some added enzymes can perform in wider pH and temperature ranges than the naturally occurring enzymes.

Adding enzymes is a common practice in Canadian distilling, and I know of a fair number of craft distillers who do it. I used to balk at the idea, just because it's not traditional. But since it doesn't seem to change the flavor or character of the whiskey, I've become more relaxed about it.

In most non-U.S. distilleries, the sugary water, now called "wort," is strained out of the grains through a false bottom in the vessel, called a "lauter tun." The false bottom sits above the real bottom and has thin slits cut in it so the wort can drain out.

The husks of the grain make an effective filter bed. Sugars left behind in the spent grains and husks are washed out with two or three "waters," fresh applications of hotter water. The initial run and the next one or two waters are collected, cooled in a heat exchanger, and sent for fermentation. The final water, the "sparge," usually becomes hydration water for the nest batch of grist, preserving the last bits of sugar (and saving the energy to heat the hydration water).

There's an additional, interesting difference in the wort at Scottish and Japanese distilleries. It has to do with turbidity or cloudiness. Most Scotch distillers pump the wort from the mash tun and get a relatively cloudy wort with some bits of the barley husks and malt flour. This will make the fermented wash have a more cereal-forward flavor, nutty, with a hint of soft baking spices. Japanese distillers and some Scottish distillers draw gently on the filter bed and get a clearer wort and a cleaner flavor in the fermented wash. They may use what's called an "underback," a separate receiving vessel that collects the wort more slowly, without drawing on the filter bed.

In American whiskey-making practice, there is no filtering, no waters. The entire mash—water, grain, husks, everything—is sent to the heat exchanger to cool, and on to the fermenter. It is called "beer" from that point on.

Since we brought up American whiskey and mash, we need to talk about sour mash. Let's go back to Rhoades, since she's something of an expert on it. She starts by talking about the acidity of the mash. "pH plays a key role during mashing," she said, "as the conversion enzymes responsible for turning starch into fermentable sugars have specific pH requirements. In the U.S. we are also allowed to modify pH, which most do (i.e., backset)."

When she says "backset," she's talking about sour mash. (It's also called "setback" by some older distillers, and no, I'm not kidding.) Modifying the acidity, the sourness, of the mash is one of the most important reasons sour mash is used. (By the way, that also answers the question, if you ever wondered about it, of why there are no sour-mash Scotches: They're not allowed to alter the pH of their water.) It also adds yeast nutrients to the mash, in the form of dead yeast.

Where does sour mash come from? The most common method is to take the leftover solids from the bottom of the still, called "slops" or "stillage," and add them to the mash. Distillers might also blend it with the grist for hydration going into the mash tun.

How does the mash get sour? Organic acids are created during fermentation. Fermentation causes acidity, and backset carries that acidity "backward" to the mashing process, where it's needed. That fermentation-created acidity is where sour mash affects the flavor of the whiskey, so we'll put that off till next chapter as well.

What about "sweet mash"? A lot of craft distillers have decided to forgo sour mash. They put only freshly made mash in the fermenter. If sour mash is so beneficial, why do sweet mash?

For one thing, tradition. Rye whiskey distillers in the pre-Prohibition era, and for a couple decades after repeal—essentially until all rye whiskey production moved to Kentucky—used a sweet mash. For another, sour mash needs to be used as quickly as possible. It's a breeding ground for lactic bacteria and can go too sour pretty quickly. You're only going to use sour mash if you're using it regularly, and a lot of smaller distillers don't mash or still every day of the week.

But another reason is that the ability of sour mash to suppress wild yeast and bacteria growth isn't as crucial or unique anymore. We'll talk more about that in the next chapter, too; but when sour mash lowers the pH of the fermenting mash, it creates an environment that gives the distiller's house yeast an advantage over the wild microbes that are about (especially in places with grain) and allows it to establish itself.

But with modern sanitation (particularly with stainless-steel fermenters) and brewing techniques, a sweet mash is much less risky these days. Get that fermenter cleaned and sanitary, cook a clean mash, and culture up a bomb-load of yeast, and the need for sour mash is minimized. It's another option distillers have, but it's no longer required.

The mash is set, it's cooled to the mid-70s Fahrenheit (mid-20s Celsius), and the yeast is ready and waiting. It's time to make some alcohol.

Ian Palmer

I talked to Ian Palmer about mashing and fermentation, and I want to thank my fellow whisky writer Dave Broom for the referral: Palmer really does know a lot about this stuff.

While I had him on the line, I picked his brain a bit about InchDairnie, his new distillery. His general plan is to stake out a space on the "whiskey flavor map," and he said, "I want to dominate that space." A specific part of that plan are his grains, so I asked a few questions about that.

Are there flavor differences between floor-malted and machine-malted barley?

"In my experience, there is no difference. But today most distilling malt is produced in very large combined germination and kilning vessels. The floor malt and the drum malt tend to be for the more specialist malts and/or smaller batches. We source from all three malting systems here at InchDairnie but all for different malts, so it is difficult to state clearly if there is a difference. You won't find the same malts being done. You're asking it to do a different job."

Does using a heritage barley, like Golden Promise, make a flavor difference?

"It always concerns me when people refer to Golden Promise as a heritage barley. When I started in the industry, this was all we used! This subject is of growing interest now, and so far there is little work on establishing the facts. Most commercial malting barleys are very similar because they come from a very restricted gene pool. Some of the older varieties behave differently in the distillery, and this will tend to result in different flavors but driven more by how they have to be handled. They will deliver a different sugar profile into the fermentation, which should then influence the fermentation.

"What I'm looking at are landrace barleys, which go further back than heritage. You will get less sugars, and a different grouping of sugars because of the starch makeup. More maltose and less maltobiose, that sort of thing. You're starting off with a different feedstock for the yeast to work with. I would expect there to be a difference, but is there going to be enough difference to notice in the new make? Maybe, but if you put it in a barrel, will there be a difference after twelve years?

"What makes it through distillation? That's a big question. You have to take a holistic view around the whole thing. What are your cereals? Your malt? What yeasts? How are you fermenting? Maybe the way you mash it enhances a flavor profile. Use a yeast that enhances that profile, then choose your cut point to enhance it. You can't think of it as one thing. You can make the most wonderful estery wash and then lose it with a bad spirit cut. It's how you put it together."

Now that's a guy who gets what we're talking about. Thanks again, Ian.

IAN PALMER

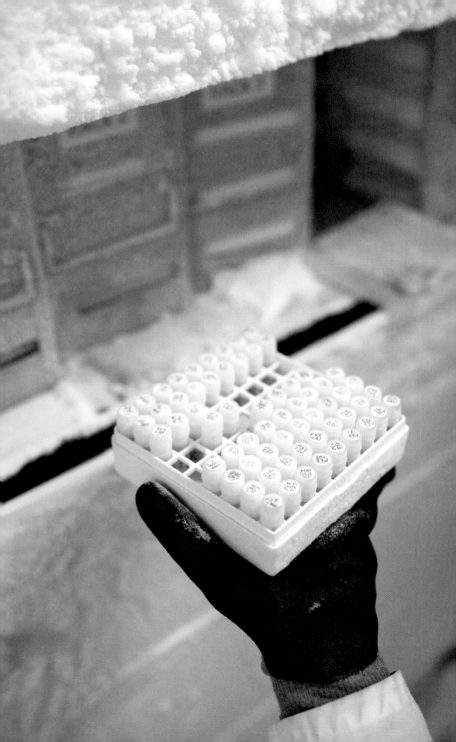

The Yeast

Yeast is the weirdest part of making whiskey. You can't get around that fact. What happens in the barrel is wrapped in some level of mystery— the "angel's share," the inescapable variety of the outcome—but I think distillers often overemphasize that, probably to soften the pain of losing so much whiskey every year.

Yeast, on the other hand, is another living thing that works with the distiller and does something the distiller simply cannot do for themselves: it makes alcohol out of grain. It's a partnership, or maybe it's something else.

I was talking about yeast to Conor O'Driscoll, the master distiller at Heaven Hill, in Louisville, Kentucky. It turned out to be his favorite topic, and he hauled out a binder that was literally 3 inches (7.6 cm) thick and started leafing through it, showing me reproduction growth curves and metabolic pathways. The two of us were chattering away (he was chattering, I was mostly taking notes and asking him to slow down) when he suddenly stopped and cocked his head.

"I wonder," he said. "Has yeast merely figured out how to get us to feed it?" There was a brief, uncomfortable silence before we both laughed. But honestly, if yeast would only churn out good whiskey for me, I'd feed it every morning and twice on Sundays.

I teased you a bit last chapter, saying that mashing wasn't really a flavor-creation step so much as a necessary preliminary to the flavor-creating steps in fermentation. Here we are, so let's look at how yeast creates not just alcohol but a rich array of flavors, aromas, and precursors that will be transformed in the barrel.

Yeast samples are preserved for years at -196°F (-127°C)

Distiller's Yeast

The yeast that distillers use for fermentation is broadly the same that brewers use for ale: Saccharomyces cerevisae. *It has been adapted to distilling by the age-old technique of maintaining the strains that worked the best, particularly ones that worked relatively quickly and weren't slowed or stunted by higher alcohol levels.*

There are many different strains of distiller's yeast, with more coming all the time. Some strains mutate quite readily.

Distillers have to be vigilant for mutations because they can quickly cause unwanted changes in flavor. That's how distillers find strains that give great flavors. Craft distillers are watching for those now, looking for the wonder yeast that gives new flavors and aromas to their whiskey.

Unlike brewers, who often harvest yeast from a current batch of beer and put it right into the next batch, distillers don't usually do that more than once or twice, largely because of the open fermentation vessels so many of them use. Open fermentation is less stressful for the yeast, but it makes contamination with wild yeast and bacteria more likely. Fresh yeast is pure yeast, so that's one way to deal with the issue.

Some distillers culture their own yeast, growing it up from samples they carefully keep cold and fresh. These are the house strains you'll hear mentioned, and bourbon distillers talk about how their predecessors kept their strain alive throughout Prohibition. Others pay a yeast laboratory to store their yeast or to provide a strain from their library. Some simply toss in cakes or bags of distiller's active dried yeast. Then there's Four Roses, where yeast is an integral part of their entire philosophy.

Yeast samples being prepared for propogation

Four Roses: The Seagram Way

Four Roses is owned by Kirin Brewery of Japan.

Before that, they were owned by Seagram; and Seagram always had a philosophy, laid down in its early years by founder Sam Bronfman, that blending was the key to consistent whiskey. Four Roses, then as now a well-respected straight bourbon, would be turned into a cheap blended American whiskey because of this obsession, though it continued to be bottled as a blend of straight bourbons for sale overseas. One of the first things Kirin did was to end the blended Four Roses and bring Four Roses bourbon home to America.

The Seagram blending philosophy lives on, though, in the distillery's now well-known process of making ten different bourbons and blending them. There are two different mashbills, each of which is then fermented by one of five distinctive yeast strains. As I'll explain later, they age the whiskeys in single-story warehouses to keep the variation of aging conditions to a minimum, focusing instead on the differences coming from the yeasts and the mashbills. After all, why go to all that trouble making ten different whiskeys only to introduce more variables?

While the flagship Four Roses will have a "mingling" of all ten whiskeys, the Small Batch bottlings have a reduced number. The Single Barrels are a rare opportunity to see just what a yeast does to a bourbon. Try two with the same mashbill but different yeasts side by side and you'll see why I've been telling you that every flavor-creating factor has to be considered.

These are the five different yeast strains, marked by their in-house letter identifier, and what they add to Four Roses' bourbons:

F: More floral, herbal, soft and full

K: Spicy, needs longer aging to develop

O: Fruity, complex, long finish

Q: Huge floral nose, quite fresh and delicate

V: A slightly fruity, well-rounded classic bourbon character

 *Four Roses
Single Barrel*

A private bottling for the Avenue Pub in New Orleans; high-rye mashbill, K yeast. It's sure enough spicy, right from the top. Clove/cinnamon, orange circus peanut candies. Splashes orange and spice and hot corn on the tongue, so lively it sings!

Dona Jugs

Some bourbon makers go a bit further when they culture their own yeast.

One of the first articles I recall reading about whiskey that was about more than "this whiskey is good, but this one is not" was a piece by bartender extraordinaire Gary Regan about "dona jugs." The dona—an odd word, maybe from the Latinate roots for "mother"—is a container and propagation vessel for yeast, in which the traditional bourbon distillers would culture up their own strains.

It was a procedure wrapped in ritual and superstitious regularity; there were special rooms, special ingredients, and certain actions that had to be performed to make the yeast come out right. The strains were kept cool in the dona jugs—in refrigerators now, but 100 years ago, the jug would be dunked in a cool well or lake. The distillers would cook up a small mash—some insisted that hops were critical to the success, while others said no—and add some of the liquid yeast to it. The yeast would grow and be transferred to another, larger vessel and fed again until it was ready to make whiskey.

The origins of the strains involved even more mystery. Distillers would leave open buckets of the special mash in particular areas outdoors—under fruit trees, by fields or streams, or their own back porch—and hope to catch a good strain of yeast. If they failed and the mash went bad, they'd try again. When they succeeded and had a yeast that smelled right, it was off to the dona.

You'd think I'd wind this up with a wink and a sigh about the old days. But this still goes on in some distilleries. It's part of the traditions of whiskey making, and it's definitely a factor in whiskey flavor.

Japanese distillers keep a variety of yeasts at the ready. As noted before, they need to have a variety of whiskies available for in-house blending, and different yeasts are a component of that strategy.

Scotch distillers, on the other hand, tend to take a very matter-of-fact approach (the major Irish distillers are generally the same). Their strains are very similar, or even identical, and apparently have been so since the 1950s. Before that, yeasts were more local, more idiosyncratic. But as breweries—a major source of yeast and yeast technology—began to consolidate, and distilleries did also, the distillers went increasingly with a single strain of yeast for the sake of convenience. Efficiency and maximum yield of alcohol were prized, and blandness became the rule, as it did in a lot of food production at that time.

Scottish distillers decided to focus on creating flavor by manipulating fermentation—temperature, time, and so on—rather than using other yeasts. I remember doing a roundtable interview with nine or ten Scotch distillery managers in the early 2000s, and not one of them was doing any experimentation with yeast. At least half of them used the same strain, and no one gave it a second thought.

It came up when I was visiting Ardbeg a few years ago for a product launch. Did the new whisky (An Oa) use any different kinds of yeast? Apparently not. "Choice of yeast," said renowned Scotch whisky blender Dr. Bill Lumsden, addressing something you could tell caused him a bit of pain, "is probably the most horribly neglected aspect of Scotch whisky."

Of course, not five minutes later, he said with a studied casualness, "That's going to be part of Project Lambic. Oh, no, I've said too much." And he *winked*. I hope he's not kidding, because a whisky made like the spontaneously fermented Lambic beers of Belgium would be fascinating indeed, and a huge leap from the current staid and stable fermentation regime of Scotch whisky.

 Allta

"Project Lambic" turned out to be Allta, which was fermented with a wild yeast found in barley fields near the distillery. Smells of bread, honey, clean sweat, and biscuit. Tastes like sweet malt and citrus, with some dry wood up front and a hint of yeasty tang on the finish.

Fermentation

Once the mash is cooled (too high a temperature will kill the yeast), the yeast is added. Each strain has different requirements for working at optimum, and distillers do what they can to provide them.

Every strain wants sugar and water (preferably slightly acidic), and they work best below 90°F (32.2°C).

Fermentation is a heat-producing reaction, so the temperature has to be monitored. If the temperature goes too low, the yeast will be stunted; too high, and the yeast will produce unwanted flavors and aromas and eventually die. Bourbon distillers used to close down over the summer, especially when demand was low. Lately more of them have chosen to spend the money to cool their fermenters rather than lose those months of production.

Yeast is also notoriously finicky about where it's working. Brewers have told me that the shape or size of the vessel can change how the yeast works. Some of that is about hydrostatic pressure on the yeast in a deeper vessel, but using forced circulation to move the liquid from bottom to top solves that problem. It's almost as if yeast has some sort of genetic memory of where it's supposed to be.

The amount of yeast that's initially put in the mash can also make a difference: A lot means a faster, cleaner fermentation; less can mean a longer, slower fermentation that may allow more wild yeast and bacteria a chance to get a foothold. Those can add their own flavors, some of them desirable, others not so much.

This is where sour mash comes in handy for American distillers, as explained in the previous chapter. According to Liz Rhoades, a senior research scientist in fermentation, distillation, and maturation for Diageo, based in Illinois, sour mash contributes to aroma formation in fermentation. "Sour mashing and lactic acid bacteria also can provide sweet, green/grassy, spicy, and meaty notes, further adding to the complexity of a whiskey."

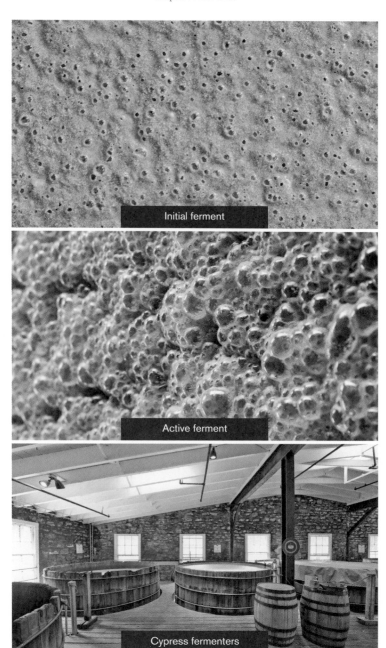

Initial ferment

Active ferment

Cypress fermenters

Chemicals versus Aromas

All the rich, sharp, delicate, and pleasing aromas that are present in whiskey are the result of chemical compounds that are created by conversion, fermentation, or autolysis; or that come from the barrel through direct absorption or through chemical transformation in various pathways created by heat, time, and oxygen transfer.

The very thought of these is stunningly complex to this former history major.

It was intimidating to think about trying to explain them to other people. I can follow the paths if they're laid out for me, but I have to be honest: I don't really understand what a carboxyl group is or the difference between an organic acid, a salt, or an ester. I do understand polymers fairly well, but that's about it.

What to do and how to handle this? Then when I was interviewing Heaven Hill's Conor O'Driscoll, I mentioned the problem to him in passing. I'd realized that to explain the presence of spicy "rye" notes in a bourbon, I'd have to explain that they were largely the effect of the presence of 4-vinyl-guaiacol (4VG), and then note that the 4VG was a derivative of the ferulic acid found in either the wheat or rye cell walls, which was broken down by yeast, but only the right yeasts, and apparently many whiskey yeasts were related to the strain brewers use for the spicy *weissbiers*…

That's where he stopped me. "Why?" he asked. "Why do you have to name the particular precursors, or the esters they produce? I'm a chemical engineer; I'd like to know that, but every time you come across a name like 4-vinyl-guaiacol, it stops the reader. You're reading, and you see that, and you stop to think about how to say it. Do you really know what it is? Why not just say there's a spicy, clove-like note, and it's from the influence of the grain and yeast?"

It made sense. I've decided to write this without getting bogged down in chemical details that I don't really understand, and probably many of the readers won't understand. (Honestly if you do understand, you can probably figure it out from the breadcrumbs I drop.)

I'm going to just name the general families of flavor and aroma compounds and what part of the process they come from: fermentation, wood extraction, oxidation, and so on. Except that thing about the ferulic acid, because that's just really cool, and I love connections between my beer-writing world and my whiskey-writing world.

Once the yeast is in the wash, or beer, it begins eating sugar and protein, and excreting alcohol, carbon dioxide (which blows off), and very important but minuscule amounts of aromatics, all while reproducing every twenty minutes or so.

That's an explosive amount of reproduction, which is how *S. cerevisiae* stays out ahead of the wild competitors and why it needs protein. Some distillers add yeast nutrients (the Scots can't), which hurry things along; but healthy yeast is, like so many other factors, more about preventing off flavors than creating new ones.

Dr. Pat Heist is the cofounder of Wilderness Trail Distillery in Danville, Kentucky. He's also the founder of Ferm Solutions, a company that provides yeast services to the industry. Heist has more than 7,000 yeast strains under refrigeration and more than 20,000 bacteria. Some have never been used for making beverage alcohol, but he keeps samples of all of them.

About those 20,000 bacteria: "You can't avoid bacterial contamination," Heist said. "Most distillers don't even track bacteria, and they're surprised when they see how much is in there. Yeast and bacteria both produce sourness but with different acids. Those acids will [react] with alcohol to create esters in the barrel."

(continued on page 83)

Aroma Compounds from Fermentation

Flavors and aromas are being created during fermentation.

Here's what's going on: Esters are fruity, aromatic by-products of fermentation that come in various flavors (e.g., isoamyl acetate: bananas; ethyl caproate: apples). Ethanol is not the only alcohol created during fermentation, even though it's usually the only one we want. It may not be the only alcohol carried over in distillation either if things aren't done right. These other alcohols may be collectively called fusel alcohols and are undesirable, oily flavors in high concentrations.

Steam-cleaning a cypress fermenter

Wooden washbacks at Springbank Distillery (Scotland)

The type of fermentation vessel can have an effect on how clean the fermentation is. If the vessel is more difficult to clean (wooden ones), bacteria is more likely to survive and affect the fermentation.

The aromatics are being produced, and what they are will depend on what strain the yeast is and what's in the tank with it. Rhoades broke it down. "Essentially the major flavors produced by yeast can be bucketed in these major flavor camps: fruity, floral, solvent/chemical, sulfur-containing, fatty/buttery, and spicy."

It's quite a range, and the trick is keeping those flavors from escaping during fermentation, and then keeping these volatiles through distillation—or not. As always, it's the distiller's choice how much of these aromas they want to keep.

But this, besides the barrel, is one of the biggest factors in flavor creation. "If you do not create the flavor foundations in the fermentation," Ian Palmer of InchDairnie Distillery said, "then they will never be in the spirit. The yeast will contribute to the different esters and many other nonethanol alcohols and other congeners, either directly or indirectly. The different yeast strains will influence the palate of flavors."

That's what we'll tackle next, in the big, meaty middle of the book: distillation, the heart of making whiskey.

Wheat Beer and Rye Whiskey

I promised you a little bit of chemistry to explain the spicy notes in rye whiskey, the peppery, clove-like edge that we find in rye whiskey and high-rye bourbon—usually.

But I've noticed that not all rye whiskeys have the same spice, and some very high-rye whiskeys indeed don't seem to have the spice at all—just the pleasant mint and grassy notes. I wondered about this for years, but I figured that somehow I wasn't getting it.

Then I called Todd Leopold at Leopold Bros. distillery in Denver for a piece on heirloom grains, and I learned something amazing about where that spice comes from. He started talking about why he was paying farmers a premium to grow Abruzzi rye for him. It's an old strain, and Leopold had read in several sources that it was the rye that used to be favored for Pennsylvania and Maryland rye whiskey production. But Abruzzi's starch content was noticeably lower than modern ryes: 62 percent compared to about 80 percent, which means less alcohol yield.

That's how commodity farmers and distillers looked at it, anyway. Leopold looked at it in reverse: 18 percent less flavorless starch meant the possibility of 18 percent more flavor. "I'm looking for older grains that have lower starch content," he said, "simply because that's a sign that there may be something else in that grain that is of interest to me as a distiller."

And that's when things took a twist. Leopold, who came to whiskey from craft brewing (and knew that I came to whiskey writing from beer writing), explained that as a brewer, he was trained how to control the spiciness found in German-style wheat beers, *hefeweizens*.

"The spicy note comes from 4-vinyl-guaiacol," he said, noting our old friend. "You control the formation of this compound by controlling its precursors…the chief of which is ferulic acid. Ferulic acid is found in some quantities in most varieties of wheat."

I asked Liz Rhoades about this, and she eagerly confirmed it. "Ferulic acid is bound within part of the cell wall material, which is greater in rye and wheat," she said. It's released during mashing, and converted to 4VG during fermentation. But, she said, "this is where yeast selection becomes critical, as not all yeast are POF+ (phenolic off note-positive). POF+ yeast strains have a specific gene that allows them to make the conversion from ferulic acid to 4VG. POF− yeasts lack this gene and cannot make the conversion."

It turns out that Abruzzi rye is loaded with ferulic acid. "When we mash 80 percent Abruzzi rye with 20 percent of our floor-malted barley," Leopold said, "I get a fermented mash that smells like the hefeweizen I made for over a decade!

"Stunning, right?" he asked, as stoked as Rhoades was by all this spicy science. "The best part is that for years distillers have believed that the classic whiskey yeast strains are descendants of hefeweizen strains. I confirmed this. The classic American and Scottish strains are nearly all POF+."

If you, like me, always thought that rye grain was responsible for the spiciness in your whiskey, it's not technically so. It's only spicy if you use the right yeast. Want proof? "Make rye bread without any added spices," Leopold said. "It's not the least bit spicy.

"This is why we use Abruzzi," he said. "Not because it's old or cool or because I believe in nostalgia. I sourced the seed and had it grown for me because the compounds in Abruzzi are very different from modern rye. Growing 'old seeds' for the heck of it is not only pointless; it's very expensive."

Hope you enjoyed the chemistry. Back to the simpler world of flavors. But that was fun, right?

Distillation

When you're making whiskey, there are a few crucial steps, things that make whiskey what it is. There's malting and mashing, which break the sugars out of dry, starchy grain. Fermentation is the natural magic that creates alcohol from those sugars, harnessing a tiny single-celled fungus to do the chemical heavy lifting. Barrel aging gives whiskey its flavor and color and rounded maturity.

These are all necessary steps, but there is one thing that sets making whiskey apart from making beer, which is otherwise what you have here, even to the barrel aging. That's distillation, the hissing, steamy science and art of separating everything that is whiskey from the beer and leaving behind that which isn't. To understand what's going on, let's go back and take a look at how distillation began and how it grew into the core concept of making whiskey. We haven't done a lot of history in the book, but it's important to understanding distillation.

Old Bushmills Distillery, in Northern Ireland (top); Wild Turkey Distillery, near Lawrenceburg, KY (bottom)

Purity of Essence

The first inklings of distillation come from the Greeks, but they seem only to have conceived of it as a way to desalinate water and perhaps make essences for fragrances. There is also archaeological evidence of possible distillation in China in the early centuries CE.

A distillery in the sixteenth century, vintage engraved illustration.

It is the Egyptians who are believed to have been the first to consistently distill alcohol. The word itself is derived from the Arabic *al-kuhl*, meaning "the kohl," the black powder used by early Egyptians for eye makeup. The etymology is uncertain, but kohl was derived by purifying metals; and it is speculated that the word spread to encompass other types of purification, including liquids like alcohol.

This was part of alchemy, the protoscience of material transformation. There is no solid evidence that alcohol was being distilled in China, Egypt, or Greece; that is, not for the purposes of recreational drinking. That would not occur until the 1400s in Ireland.

Distillation came to Ireland by way of Christian monks. Along with their faith and a desire to live holy lives in isolation from Europe's wars and dynastic politics, these monks brought with them an amazing amount of knowledge; mathematics and science gleaned from many sources. Judging from what soon came after, that knowledge included some of the texts of the Arab and Egyptian alchemists who were distilling and rectifying centuries before.

From the evidence in the records that survive, those philosophers were distilling for reasons other than refreshment: science, medicine, perfumery. All good reasons, to be sure, but the monks found the use that would turn distillation into a cultural phenomenon and profitable enterprise.

We don't know how these monks came to distill strong spirits from beer and then get the idea of drinking it in more than slight medicinal doses. The first mention of it we have dates from the early 1400s. This would have been pot-stilled spirit made from a malt beer, almost certainly unaged, more than likely flavored with herbs, flowers, perhaps honey. We don't know if the monks knew about making the cuts as the spirit began to flow from the condensing arm, but the awful smell of the undesirable heads and tails should have quickly led to an understanding of what "the good stuff" was.

From these small, rudimentary beginnings would grow a knowledge that quickly spread across the mere 12 miles (19.3 km) of water to Scotland and the monastic communities there. There is a 1494 record from a Scottish monastery of the purchase of malt to make *aqua vitae. Aqua vitae*, or "water of life/vitality," was the Latin name the alchemists gave this spirit. The Gaelic translation, *uisce beatha*, would become—after enough years of drinking it—linguistically massaged to "whiskey."

Soon farmers would gain the knowledge as well and have a new use for their crops. All it took

was some copper and a bit of skill to hammer out a riveted vessel, and a farmer was now a distiller.

The benefits of whiskey over beer were clear. Whiskey didn't sour or go bad and wouldn't freeze. It wasn't just a drink; it was a fire starter, liniment, cleanser, and medicine. It took up less volume and was much more valuable in trade. So much more valuable, in fact, that the whiskey a farmer made and sold could mean the difference between a reasonable profit and mere survival for his family.

Distillation was truly a disruptive technology. It took agricultural products that were millennia old—beer, wine, cider—and made something completely new out of them. We had to learn how to make it and how to safely drink it (in a chemical heads and tails sense; we're still working on the dosage part). We also had to learn how to incorporate it into national economies. Distilled spirits, once people learned what they were, created not just new industries but new sources of government revenue.

As is still the case today, the dance of taxation and licensing would bring about changes in whiskey and changes in distillation. Change what is taxed—malt, or the size or number of stills used by a distillery, for instance—and you will almost certainly change how people make their whiskey, if they can see a way to pay less in taxes.

British taxation sought out the growing spirits industry like a profit-seeking missile. There wasn't a reliable method of gauging the amount of alcohol being produced, so alternative measures were put to use. In the late 1770s, for example, the government initiated taxing distillers' production based on the volume of the wash stills, the large pot stills used in the first distillation of the beer or wash. Distillers responded by building their stills with the same volume, but much wider and shallower, so the wash would boil quicker and they could run more batches in a day, producing well beyond government estimates.

The whiskey in these big stills, run in Ireland and Lowland Scotland, suffered from a hard-driven distillation, losing more volatiles and flavor. That made the product of the illegal "sma' stills" (small stills) back in the Highlands even more prized once it got to market illegally.

A tax on malt in the United Kingdom was intended to bypass the failings of the still tax. Tax the grain used to make the whiskey, and size of the still doesn't matter. As we've seen earlier, this was the origin of mixed-mash single pot still Irish whiskey: using less malt to make the same amount of whiskey.

(It still happens. Increased whisky taxes in the United Kingdom led the Scotch whisky industry to focus more on the export market. A tax break for including American ingredients led to greater innovation in Canadian blended whiskies.)

Meanwhile, a revolution was beginning in whiskey distillation (and Armagnac distillation, right around the same time). This was the continuous, or column, still. The main limit, the bottleneck of a pot still, is that it is a batch device. Put in a charge of wash, distill it until it's done, clean the still, and run the next batch.

But what if you could just continuously pour wash into the still, heat it, and get a constant stream of spirits? In the early 1800s, fuels, metallurgy, and physical chemistry all reached a point where such a still became possible. Different spirits industries used it in different ways, but the column still became the accepted alternative to the pot still: more efficient, capable of easily distilling to a higher proof, and still able to produce a flavorful spirit.

At that point, distillation processes were largely set, though the craft distillers are busily tinkering around the edges again, this time more for aesthetic reasons than for those of economics. Let's take a wide view of how whiskey distillation works before moving on to specific stills in the next two chapters.

Boiling Points

At the heart of distillation is a simple, basic difference between two liquids' physical properties.

The reason we can make whiskey is because alcohol (ethanol) boils at 173.1°F (78.4°C) and water boils at 212°F (100°C). Distillers use this difference to separate the two. Put beer (whether you call it "beer" or "wash") in your still (whether it's a pot or a column), heat it to the boiling point of alcohol, and then capture the vapors that come off the boiling liquid. Condense them and—ta-da!—you have alcohol.

If only it were that easy. The process is never that precise and clean, and physically never can be. The amount of time it takes to heat all the alcohol past evaporation (which takes more heat out of the mix as it happens), the swirling differences in heat and pressure within the still, and mostly the physical chemistry of boiling two liquids in solution all have an effect; and it leads to a separation that is less than clean and precise.

But thank the dumb luck of humans, who live in a universe of physical laws we never made for that dirty imprecision. If it *were* that easy, if fractional distillation of wash into

alcohol and everything else were something precise and clean and simple, there would be no whiskey. There would only be vodka, gin, aquavit, and the like rolling out of the still at a constant 95 percent ABV (physical chemistry dictates that you cannot distill pure alcohol; just can't do it). Not a terrible world, but it wouldn't be as fine as this whiskey-filled one we have.

Worst of all, it would be a terrible waste of all the flavor we just spent the past three chapters building!

The distillation process has several goals, most of which are made possible by this manipulation of boiling points. Starting with your—let's just call it "beer," for simplicity's sake—at somewhere between 7 percent and 15 percent alcohol, roughly, the main goal is to get it up to somewhere between 65 percent and 80 percent alcohol. If you're making blended whiskey, you'll want it cranked all the way up to about 92 percent. That's Job One.

(continued on page 94)

Man versus Machine

Some distilleries have "digital probes" and "servo-actuated valves" run from a computerized control room. Others are worked by hand and eye and sweat and memory. Is one way better?

The relative merits of automation are a settled argument in most industries. Automation saves money, increases efficiency, and makes for a consistent product. But in the distilling business, tradition often trumps efficiency. Whiskey makers differ on the amount of automation they'll allow in the process, and they have good arguments for both sides.

Consider the case for automation. Wire your system with probes, switches, actuators. Record everything as the distillery workers make a batch of spirit from milling to distillation: temperatures, times, yeast counts, pH, alcohol levels, and so on. Test every batch of spirit as it comes off the final distillation.

When you find the runs that have come out the best, program your control system to re-create that run every time. You have now consistently repeated a great distillation run. You may miss the possibility of the occasional incredible run, but you've eliminated every one that might be below average.

And even when the machines are opening and closing, stirring and steaming, they're still mimicking what a very human person decided and did.

On the other hand, if your process is automated, do the people pushing the buttons from a control room know why they're pushing those buttons? The team that's working in the manually operated brewery and stillhouse knows what's going on, because they can smell it, they hear it, they feel the heat and the vibration. They've become attuned to the whole thing, and that, supporters argue, makes better whiskey and can improve it.

Can they make mistakes? Sure, they can make some; but making whiskey, even for experienced people with a long-settled regimen, is a process fraught with chaotic elements. Barrels are handmade, and they may come to the distiller from a variety of sources. Grain varies; not as much as grapes do for a vintner, but it's there. The weather can affect mashing and fermentation; climate affects aging.

The whiskey will age differently in various warehouses or on different floors of the same warehouse. The blender has to bring it all together; what's one more random factor, really?

Once again, to automate or not, and any level in between, is not better or worse but just another choice for the distillers and their whiskey.

MAN VERSUS MACHINE

Bottling lines benefit from automation

Getting there means leaving a lot of water behind. That's the second goal: taking out what we don't want. We certainly don't want all that water; if we did, we'd be brewers. But there are other things we don't want. There are unhealthy compounds—some directly toxic, some that have a cancer risk. These are easily, almost automatically removed though, so don't worry.

There are compounds that are simply unpleasant—meaty, heavy, sulfury aromas, smells of paint thinner and nail polish remover—that can be revolting in high concentrations, though some can add bracing body and structure in small amounts. These bad smells are removed through careful control of the distillation process and by the plentiful presence of chemically reactive copper in the shell and guts of the stills (and condensers) themselves.

The third main goal of distillation is to capture and keep the flavors that have been carefully built up over the stages of malting, mashing, and fermenting. These are the things that drive distillation, that feed the still. Distillery brewers have to

consistently hit those marks to give the stillman the right materials to work with.

The problem is that the boiling points of those volatile compounds, the good ones and the bad ones, are scattered above and below the boiling point of alcohol. Distillers (and to some extent, the designer of the still) have to understand where those points are and how to work with them and the limitations of the still to keep what they want, cut or leave behind what they don't, and keep the spirit interesting, all while running the still as efficiently as possible.

Three goals, then: Concentrate the alcohol, remove the water and foul components, and preserve the desirable flavors, all in consistent proportions from run to run. No matter what kind of still you're using, no matter what complex or simple setup you have, those three goals remain the same.

Horses for Courses

If you've looked at the table of contents, you know that there are three chapters on distillation.

The two following this one are specific to the types of stills: one for pot stills and one for columns and other types. Obviously we'll dive deeper into still types in those chapters, but here is the place to note that the type of still is yet another choice.

Stills are a means to an end, hitting those three goals mentioned previously. The choice of still for each national tradition is largely just that—traditional. Bourbon can be made in a pot still. Scotch and Irish grain whiskeys are made in column stills, and you can make malt whiskey in a column still that could almost certainly pass as pot-stilled single malt Scotch in a blind tasting. The Japanese use both types, and the Canadians use a variety of stills.

But each tradition has its own rules, guidelines, and expectations for how distillation is to be done. All of them make whiskey, and all of them can make excellent whiskey. We won't be saying "This still is better," or "This still is for making bulk whiskey." We'll be having a look at how each still adds—and removes—flavor.

FEW Spirits (Evanston, IL) went from a hybrid still to the beer still shown here.

How the Midleton Stills Almost Killed Me

About ten years ago, I was at a press event at Midleton Distillery, the big Irish Distillers facility where Jameson and Redbreast, among others, are made.

It was a huge event, and I was touring the distillation hall with twenty other journalists. David Quinn, the affable and astute head of whiskey science for Irish Distillers, was explaining all the possible paths for the distillate to take among the variety of stills.

It was dizzying. The heads cuts of a pot still run of single pot still might go into the next run, or they might be split and part of them sent to a column still; the tails cuts might be redistilled immediately with partial cuts from the previous week; the hearts cut on the first spirit run could be split among three different stills for redistillation … look, any further and I'd be making it up because I was lost at this point. Quinn was pointing at multiple junctures of pipes well over our heads!

I looked around in desperation, and there's whisky writer Dave Broom, coolly leaning against the railing, not taking any notes at all. He noticed my panic and smiled. "Don't worry," he said, in that purling Glaswegian ripple he has. "There'll be a whole PowerPoint deck on this." Of course there would be. I relaxed.

Explanation over, we began to move on, and I made my way to Quinn's side. "Is there a handout for that?" I asked. "Could you send me one?"

He cocked an eye at me and said, very seriously, "On paper? No, why do you think I was talking so fast? If I thought you'd actually followed me and got all that down, I'd have to kill you." And he moved on to the front of the group.

I like Quinn. We've always gotten along, but I'm still not sure if he was joking. Suffice to say, the possibilities presented by a large number of stills and a will to experiment are substantial, and most distillers only ever scratch the surface. Midleton has to press those boundaries because of the same lack of blending partners the Japanese distillers have.

For now, let's home in on how a still works. The common threads of the process run through all types of stills. The beer comes in and is usually preheated as it goes into the still to make the boiling quicker. This will often take place in a heat exchanger that simultaneously cools the vapors or the leftovers from the previous batch. The beer goes into the still, and the heating and separating begin.

The first run for the pot still takes hours, as gallons and gallons of beer have to boil. Columns take a couple minutes for the beer to make its way through the still. As the vapors rise, steamy and laced with alcohol and flavors, they rub up against the copper in the still and leave some of their stuff behind. That's where some nastiness goes away. The water and grain residue are left behind.

Some of the vapors run out of energy, literally, then condense and fall back into the still. That's called "reflux," and it's part of keeping some flavors out and letting others through, because it can be tuned and tweaked—and that's a lot of the effects of having the pot stills in different shapes and having cooling jackets at the top of stills.

When the vapors do escape, they go to a condenser. From there the liquid will go either to a second (or third) pot still, or to the doubler (or thumper)—or whatever is being used for this spirit—and be distilled again. This run cleans things up a lot more. Then it's another run through the condenser, and we're done. That's new make, ready to be proofed and poured into a barrel.

Pretty simple. Heat beer to boiling, extract the alcohol and aromatic compounds you want from the water and grain bits and leave the others behind, run the vapors past a lot of copper (to pull off more nasty stuff), and condense them to liquid. Then boil it again, lose more undesirable components, condense this good vapor, and you're done. Different distillers do different things with the leftovers: They may become sour mash, they may become animal feed, or they may be burned off. And that's it.

The Still Makers

Most of the large stills (and some smaller ones) in America are made by Vendome, a family-owned company that has been located in Louisville's Butchertown neighborhood for more than 100 years.

Vendome Copper and Brass Works makes both column and pot stills, mash cookers, doublers and thumpers—I've even seen their black-and-brass nameplate on brewing equipment occasionally.

A good number of the craft distillers in America use hybrid pot-and-column stills made by the German manufacturer CARL (formerly Christian Carl). They've been making stills in Eislingen for more than 150 years. Quite a few eau-de-vie distillers in Europe use their stills.

The big name in Scotch whisky stills is Forsyths. The Forsyths works in Rothes makes and maintains pot stills, column stills, fermenters, condensers, tanks, and all the copperwork you require for making whisky. They sell to distillers in America as well, and they also make heavy equipment and fittings for the oil and gas industry in the North Sea.

Huge sheets of copper fill the sheds at each plant, and the pounding sound of hammering, the hiss of welding torches, and the whine of drills fill the air.

There are few standard configurations at Forsyths because every change in a pot still changes the flavor. No one wants to be the same. The column stills change in size at Vendome, depending on how much whiskey you think you'll need to make. Designs change at CARL, depending on how flexible you want your still to be; they make stills for eau-de-vie distillers, which are very tight on the cuts. But a distiller may want to be able to make a fat, funky rum as well.

The still is the heart of a whiskey-making operation. Without it, you've got a brewery and a bunch of empty warehouses. It's worth the money to get the best.

Heat exchanger and pot still being built at Vendome.

Making It Work

If this is distilling, what does the "master distiller" do? Is that the term you're familiar with? It's used at some places, but others have a distillery manager, a distiller, an operations manager, a brewer, and a stillman. But someone makes the decisions about when to make the cuts, about how much sour mash to put in the newly set mash for fermentation, when to add more cooling water in the summer, and when to turn up the steam.

A lot of that job gets done by rote. You turn things on because it's time to turn them on; you do it because the saccharometer indicates that fermentation is complete. But other things get done because the still just sounds right, because the liquid coming out of the pipe is clear and doesn't smell cheesy, or because it feels slick between your fingertips. Distillation is a science with numbers and energy and temperature changes; but distillation is also an art, which is why there are always people on the job.

You'll see a saying in a few chapters: "You can't sneak up on a stillman." That's because as they get more experienced and used to their job, they know what the machinery is going to sound like at every stage,

and any sound that's out of place will trigger their alertness. The same thing will happen with strange smells in the brewery, the fermentation hall, or the warehouse. Warehouse managers will tell you they don't smell the whiskey at all anymore— which seems mad, because to the casual visitor it's a wonderful rich bath of vanilla, oak, and fruit—but if something's off, they'll smell it immediately.

People get the job done in distillation. Stills are tools, but people run them. Let's move on to the next chapter and see how pot stills perform in the hands of the masters.

The Pot Still

Chapter 7:

The two vintage pot stills at Michter's Fort Nelson Distillery (Louisville, KY)

When the discussion of distillation turns to the difference between making whiskey with pot stills and column stills, there is always the temptation to come up with a neat analogy that will make everything clear. They tend to be a bit subjective. Following are some fresh ones I made up for you:

Using a pot still is like doing crochet by hand; a column still is like using an automated sewing machine.

Using a pot still is like driving a sports car; a column still is like driving a truck.

Using a pot still is like cooking a meal from scratch; a column still is like cooking with a microwave.

Get the picture? The general idea seems to be that making whiskey with a pot still is the real thing, the way it's supposed to be done. There are definitely people in Kentucky who disagree with that (and some folks making good grain whisky in other places), but pot stills are linked indelibly with the idea of hand-making good whiskey.

If you look at whiskey history, as we did in the previous chapter, that connection is easy to understand. The pot still is how things started hundreds of years ago, after all; and in an industry that practically shrink-wraps and sells *tradition* by the portion, that goes a long way.

All I'm selling are thoughts and ideas, though, so let's take a closer look at just what a pot still can do in terms of creating and refining whiskey flavor. We're mostly going to be looking at Scotland because of the sheer number of distillers using pot stills and the well-established history. There are, of course, pot stills being used in all the major distilling areas, but they're mostly used in similar ways.

Like a Pot

That's why a pot still is called that, after all. It's because that's what it looks like, and that's how it works, like a pot on the fire. Do this: Go to your kitchen, fill a pot about one-third full of water. Put the lid on the pot, and then put it on the heat to boil. After the water boils, lift the lid—carefully!— and take a look at the underside. It's covered in water. That's condensed steam, and that's exactly how a pot still works.

Well, almost exactly. For one thing, you'd have "wash" in the pot (as the Scots call the beer they make into whisky) instead of water, and that would be condensed water and alcohol on the "lid." As we discussed in the previous chapter, the difference in boiling points of these liquids (and the other flavors in the wash) is what makes distillation possible.

But the other difference is just as important: You need an outlet, an exit for those alcohol vapors to get out of the pot. Otherwise, they'll just keep condensing and falling back in (remember that reflux thing?) and escaping around the very loose seal of your pot lid until you have nothing left but a scorched, stinking pot.

So a pot still is built with a rounded bottom and a tapered neck on top. The vapors go up and exit at the top of the still, usually a 90-degree or so bend into the "lyne arm," the tube that leads the vapors away to the condenser. This is where all resemblance to boiling water in a pot ends, but it was useful to our initial envisioning of the process.

In the first distillation in pot stills, the "wash run," the wash is going from the low alcohol concentration of beer, between 7 percent and 15 percent, roughly, and leaving the water behind to bring the concentration of alcohol between 20 percent and 25 percent.

This is pretty straightforward, just leaving a lot of water (plus small grain bits and a tiny, unrecoverable amount of alcohol) behind as alcohol and flavor are captured. The liquid left behind, the "pot ale," is disposed of (sometimes as a cattle-feed additive).

Once the vapors from the wash run have condensed (they're now called "low wines"), they'll be sent to the spirit still, combined with leftovers from previous spirit runs, and distilled again. This time the distillation will be carefully monitored, and the first rush of liquid from the condensers—called the "heads" or "foreshots"—will be diverted and captured for redistillation in the next run. There is alcohol in here, and the distiller wants to

capture it. But there are undesirable compounds as well, and they'll have to be further transformed through distillation or disposed of.

Once these undesirables have run out and the spirit runs clean (almost all alcohol), a "cut" is made and the liquid is now sent to a holding tank reserved for new make spirit. There will be a lengthy run to capture as much of this "heart cut" as possible. A tight, short heart cut leaves out more of the sharper and heavier flavors. A broader, longer cut will leave in more of the nonalcohol elements, called "congeners," giving the spirit a deeper, somewhat oily character.

The next change in the character of the liquid is the cut that redirects the "tails" or "feints." The feints are saved like the heads and blended back into the next set of low wines, the next "charge," for redistillation. Once there is no alcohol coming over in the feints, the remainder of the liquid in the spirit still, called the "spent lees," is disposed of.

That's how a full whisky run on pot stills works. But that's similar to telling you how to drive a car by telling you to turn the key, shift into Drive, move the wheel to steer, and press the brakes to stop. We've said nothing about manual transmissions, trucks, sports cars, SUVs, or off-road vehicles; we've said nothing about turbochargers, all-wheel drive, snow tires, or changing the factory-standard computer chip. Or, for that matter, directions, speed limits, and the other cars on the road.

Pot stills are almost insanely adjustable. We're going to take a look at that and, of course, how it affects flavor.

Partially Potted

You may think you need to buy from a small-run craft distillery or Woodford Reserve to get pot still–made bourbon. All the other bourbon is made on a column still, right?

Well, yes—and no—because almost all of the big distillers use pot stills for a second run after the column. You may have heard of them as the *doubler*.

The doubler isn't generally batch fed like a regular spirit pot still, although that can be done. The stream of rough spirit off the column's condenser dumps into the pot, which is steam heated. The alcohol-rich vapor passes out through a lyne arm, and water and impurities are left behind in the pot. The alcohol level of the spirit doesn't rise that much; it's mainly a purification run.

A couple distillers use a simplified version of a pot still, called a thumper. It's a simple chamber about two-thirds full of water. The hot vapors off the column are fed directly into the water, coming out below the surface. The compression of the vapor as it hits the water causes a thumping sound. The constant addition of heat from the vapor boils the liquid. The vapor that comes out the top has left impurities and water behind, leaving it cleaner and a bit higher in alcohol. It passes on to a condenser and becomes the new make.

No one who does this calls their spirit "pot stilled." They're proud to be distilling on a column. But they use the pot to put the finishing touches on the spirit.

A copper still at the Ardnahoe Distillery in Islay, Scotland

PARTIALLY POTTED

Tweaking the Pot

The first thing you notice about pot stills, once you've seen a few, is that you don't often see ones that look alike. There are easily explained differences: Wash stills are bigger than spirit stills because they have to contain a much larger volume of liquid. But we've got bulging balls and skinny necks and all kinds of things going on.

Is this just decorative? Of course not; it's about flavor. The stand-out observations are about relative sizes and ratios, the "still geometry" as I like to call it. Some stills are broad and squat, while some are tall and lean. Some distillers have one fairly large wash still, where others may have a few smaller ones. You may see a distiller that has increased capacity by copying the existing stills in painstakingly exact larger ratios.

Why does still geometry matter? It's about reflux and copper. Reflux occurs as the wash boils and vapor rises in the pot. When the boil has just begun, the neck is not fully heated and the vapor will condense on the cooler metal of the neck and run back into the base of the still; it's looking like our cooking pot again.

As the still becomes fully heated, the vapors reach higher and higher before condensing. Eventually they make it to the exit and into the lyne arm.

What's the point of reflux? Think of it as heavy and light balls in a pit. We want the lighter balls to go into another pit, while leaving the heaviest ones behind. So we start vibrating the floor of the pit rapidly up and down, bouncing the balls, adding energy to their flight—the equivalent of adding heat to the spirit still.

The lighter balls bounce higher. The lightest ones—the compounds with the lower boiling temperatures—will escape the pit first, while the heavier ones are still bouncing off the walls and falling back into the pit. Some of the heavier balls may bounce pretty high, but as long as we keep an eye on things and dial back the energy when they start getting too close, they'll stay in there. Eventually the lighter balls will all bounce out, and some of the medium-weight balls will come out as well, leaving the heaviest ones inside. This is a middle-run spirit, fairly standard.

Now say we decide we want a lighter spirit: only the lighter balls. We raise the walls of the pit, making it less likely for the heavier balls to escape. That's the equivalent of a taller still making a more floral, "elegant" spirit.

Conversely, a squat, short-necked still allows more of the heavy components into the spirit: a bit sulfury, some of the flavors we call "meaty," a spirit with some chew to it. We've lowered the walls of the pit, making it easier for more of the balls to bounce out.

In our ball-pit analogy, the first, lightest balls out are the heads, and we'll scoop them up and keep them for next time because there are a few good medium-weight balls in there that "got lucky" and escaped. When the balls are coming out the fastest, in the middle, that's the hearts. The last balls out are the tails, and we'll put them back in the next time to recapture the few slow-moving medium-weight balls.

The height of the still changes the reflux, but that's not the only way to do it. Tall and slim causes even more reflux, as the vapor is more likely to hit the copper; tall and wide, there's less contact and the vapor keeps moving. A still may have a kind of wasp-waisted constriction at the base of the neck (called a "lamp-glass" still); that gives some separation between the vapor and the active surface of the wash. It gives a smoother flow that pushes against the copper walls. A bulge at the bottom of the neck—a boil ball—also slows down the vapor flow to create more reflux.

(continued on page 110)

Strange Stuff

Some distilleries using pot stills are simply straight-up normal. Wash still, spirit still, boil the wash, run the low wines, redistill the heads and tails, send the new make to the spirit receiver—done. The stills may be shaped in their own ways, but they use the standard repertoire of tall, short, lamp-glass constriction or boil-ball bulb.

Then there are the other distilleries, with other ideas. A small handful, for instance, put a water jacket on the necks of the spirit stills, keeping them cooler to increase reflux. The hot vapors never get a chance to heat the copper of the neck, resulting in greater fallback, and a lighter spirit.

The Dalmore has water jackets and also has flat-topped stills (the story is they were cut off and capped to fit under a floor above) that seem to increase reflux. They run four wash stills and four spirit stills in what stillman Mark Hallas told me was "an unbalanced distilling system." Over twenty-four hours of careful, manually controlled distilling, the size of the wash runs and the capacity of the spirit stills balance out. Hallas had no time for automation and didn't think a machine could run his stills properly. "You need the people," he said, and flashed a quick grin as he tapped the side of his head. "The meat in the machine."

Japan's two big distillers are limited in their ability to trade whiskies for making blends (largely because they don't really have a working relationship). So each one has a menagerie of stills making an array of spirits in order to get the variety they need. Canadian distillers are in somewhat the same boat and also have deliberately different stills. Irish distillers have similar stills to Scottish distilleries, but as I noted in the previous chapter, they're quite innovative in their use. Some of the newer Irish distilleries are resurrecting designs from the past; I saw an interesting almost-spherical still at the new Tullamore distillery.

Almost all pot stills run on wash, but there are some that distill "on grain," like the column stills in Kentucky. Woodford Reserve, for instance, runs their bourbon mash right into their wash still and has to clean and pump it out every run. Up in Iceland, Flóki makes a malt whisky that's distilled on grain, and it gives the new make an interesting hint of dry cocoa.

STRANGE STUFF

And then there's Mary, at the A. Smith Bowman Distillery in Virginia. Though run as a batch-process spirit still, Mary is really a doubler, designed to do the second distillation on column-distilled bourbon. For decades, the Bowman distillery has bought low wines from Kentucky distillers and run them through Mary to make their whiskey.

Mary is a wide, straight-sided copper cylinder, topped with a constricted boil ball that leads straight up to a spiral lyne arm that goes through about three and a half turns before finally leading to the condenser. I've never seen anything like Mary in more than twenty years of writing about whiskey.

"Mary" at A. Smith Bowman Distillery (Fredericksburg, VA)

STRANGE STUFF

It doesn't even have to be about the body of the still itself. Running the spirit still at a barely boiling temperature will give a longer distillation and lead to greater reflux.

Some lyne arms have a slight upward tilt to them, and condensing vapor will run back down into the pot again; a sharper downward tilt, and you make it a bit easier for the vapor to get away (i.e., less reflux).

The easiest way to increase reflux, of course, is to add another run through the spirit still. Triple distillation is done at the big Irish distilleries—Midleton, Bushmills, and Tullamore—but it's also done at Auchentoshan in Scotland. Springbank triple distills their Hazelburn whisky. Triple distillation makes for a lighter spirit because of that increased reflux.

There are also idiosyncratic add-ons to stills that recirculate part of the vapors directly back into the stills. Ardbeg has one they call the "purifier." It's described as a "semicondenser" on the spirit still's lyne arm, which returns some spirit to the pot. They

believe it adds citrus character to the spirit. There's no cooling water in it; the vapor condenses due to the pressure drop. "We ran some spirit once with the purifier offline," recalled renowned Scotch whisky blender Dr. Bill Lumsden recalled. "It was like 'Ardbeg Big & Chunky.'"

To reinforce, more reflux means a cleaner, more elegant spirit, a lighter spirit with more floral and fruit and citrus aromas. Less reflux means a heavier, more gutsy spirit, with a bit of chew to it, that "meaty" character that some of us prize. Both of those can come through aging in interesting ways, delicious ways. Reflux is terrifically important to the flavor, body, and aging profile of whiskey.

Reflux also increases the amount of contact with copper, and as we've mentioned before, copper cleans up the whiskey. Everywhere hot spirit touches hot, clean copper, the whiskey gets cleaner. That's the main reason that stills (and pipes, worm tubs, and shell-and-tube condensers) are made of copper. Steel would last much longer and be cheaper in the long run. It's just that copper makes whiskey better than any metal we've yet found.

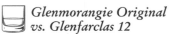 *Glenmorangie Original vs. Glenfarclas 12*

A tale of two mouthfeels. Glenmorangie's tall stills: Light, a tongue dancer, delicate. Glenfarclas's squat stills: Full bodied, palate coating, long finish. Both delightful.

Copper Chemistry

Copper pot stills and copper column stills are gorgeous when they're gleaming and polished.

But they're prone to dents, they wear out quickly and have to be repaired, and even when they're working, they get tarnished. And you know some low-tenure stillman is going to wind up polishing them, by hand. Yet distillers are in love with copper. What's the story?

"Originally copper was used because it was available," Dr. Bill Lumsden told me. "It was malleable, you could shape it fairly easily into the shape of a still, and it had good heat transfer capability. It was by chance that it was discovered that the copper chemically reacts with the condensing vapors." It happened after fabricators learned how to make affordable stainless-steel stills—and learned a few years later that they made awful whiskey.

It comes down to chemistry. Freshly cleaned copper reacts with sulfur compounds in the vapor—the sulfur comes from the grains—to create copper sulfate. The black, noxious-smelling compound stays behind and the spirit flows clean.

Without copper? "[The whiskey] would be very pungently sulfury, meaty, almost a cabbagey smell," said Lumsden. "Not really what you would want. Not only would there be too much of the sulfur itself; it would mask a lot of the fruitiness and subtlety of the whiskey."

Chemistry is wonderfully serendipitous like that sometimes. It's also somewhat romantic in this case. When copper binds to the sulfur, it uses up the metal, thinning the stills, the condensers, the lyne arm; everything copper eventually has to be replaced, all because it literally gives itself away to make our whiskey taste better. We say the best people have hearts of gold; the best whiskeys have shiny souls of copper.

Heating and Cooling

How the still is heated makes a difference. Back in the early days, every still was heated the same direct way—you built a fire under it.

It may have been in a brick firebox or a simple turf fire around a crofter's secret sma' still back in the glens, but fire was on the copper. This is called "direct fire." It started as turf or wood, then coal and fuel oil, and now the few distillers still doing direct fire using natural gas.

Direct fire had disadvantages. It is harder on the copper, inside and out. On the outside, there are

deposits from the fire, so the fire had to be carefully tended. On the inside, sugars would caramelize on the copper where the sugars in the wash hit the hot metal. Distillers came up with a solution to the caramelization. They built geared arms into the stills that would turn as the wash boiled. The arms dragged heavy nets of coiled copper links, called "rummagers." The rummagers scrape the caramel

Worm tubs at Talisker Distillery (Scotland)

off, and it remains in the wash to add flavor to the spirit.

Almost every distiller in Scotland (and, to the best of my knowledge, everywhere else) has transitioned to steam heat for their stills. It's cleaner, there's no need for rummagers (with their added expense and wear on the stills), and it makes for an even heat. A couple distillers stick to direct fire, though, because of the flavor it adds to their whisky.

There's one last consideration in the pot still, and that's how the spirit vapors get cooled. There are two types of condensers used in making Scotch whisky. Worm tubs are the old-style coiled copper tubes immersed in cool water, familiar to anyone who's seen pictures of moonshine stills. The other, more modern type, is called shell-and-tube, where a couple hundred copper tubes turn back and forth inside a copper shell. There is cold water running through the tubes; the shell is filled with the vapor from the stills.

The shell-and-tube condensers expose the vapor to a lot more copper and cool the vapor more quickly and efficiently. The worm tubs work more slowly and with less copper exposure. As you might expect, the worm tubs make for a heavier spirit. And as you can guess, that's another case of not

being better or worse, but another choice for creating flavor in whisky.

Pot stills represent perhaps the most tradition-bound part of the industry. When a distiller has a certain shape (or shapes) of still, and a particular way of running it, they will want to stick with that forever. I remember asking someone at The Glenlivet why their stills were in the shape they were, looking for an answer that would indicate some kind of planning for what they were making. He told me they were that way because that's the way they'd always been. You do it the same way, whatever the reason was originally, because that's how your spirit is made.

Now about that idea that pot stills make better whiskey: the next chapter is the column still's rebuttal. I'll see you there.

 Talisker 10

Talisker's big worm tubs are cooled with sea loch water. You'll get a smack of smoke right away; dive in to taste a boldly burly blend of peat smoke, seaweed, and black pepper, buoyed by a fat malt cushion.

The Column Still

Chapter 8:

It's a tough call on what aspect of whiskey making is more misunderstood: the composition and quality of blended whiskey or the use and limitations of the column still. Blended whiskey gets a bad rap from a lot of single malt snobs and, sadly, the column still gets the same treatment. We'll talk more about blended whiskey's underappreciated beauty later. Let's settle the column still misunderstanding right now.

First what do you picture when I say "column still"? There are at least two types in current, everyday use in making whiskey: the Coffey still and the Kentucky beer still. The Coffey still, patented in the United Kingdom in 1831 by Aeneas Coffey (a former exciseman, ironically), is an improvement on the features of stills developed by several previous inventors that revolutionized the distillation of beverage alcohol. The Kentucky beer still takes the "analyzer" column of Coffey's still and runs it by itself, with a condenser to cool the vapors and a second pot still–like device to clean the distillate.

Let me make a confession right now: I'm an American, and I cut my whiskey-drinking *and* whiskey-writing teeth on bourbon. American-style distilling tends to color the way I think about distilling in some cases. The reason I bring this up is because when I hear the words "column still," I tend to automatically picture the Kentucky beer still.

I have been working on correcting that in preparation for writing this chapter. I suspect that there are a number of people out there on either side of this regional distillation fence who have the same prejudice. If you think you might, keep an open mind.

To understand the difference between the two and understand column stills, in general, we'll have to get into some details (and illustration). You may have heard that a column still works like a series of stacked pot stills. I don't believe that image is sufficiently correct to be useful. I find it easier to do a very simple walk-through of the column, following the path of the wash (in American distillation, this would be "beer").

In Coffey's still, the cool wash arrives at the top of the second column, called "the rectifier," and travels downward through it, in a series of looped pipes. It is heated as it drops by the hot vapor from the first column, "the analyzer."

This hot wash is now fed into the top of the analyzer. The wash drops through a series of perforated plates as pressurized steam enters at the bottom and rises, heating the wash and taking the alcohol with it as vapor. The vapor exits the top of the column and goes to the bottom of the analyzer.

As the hot vapor rises through the analyzer, it heats the wash in the looped pipes. This cools the vapor and causes reflux. The liquid that drops out and falls to the bottom well of the analyzer is pumped to the rectifier and fed in near the top to run through again. The vapor that continues to rise passes through a "spirit plate" near the top. Once it makes it through the spirit plate, either it cools and is collected to the condenser and spirit well, or it passes out through the top as vapor and is condensed and returned to the incoming cool wash. The cycle continues to run as long as wash and steam enter the still. Periodically the still is shut down for cleaning and maintenance.

The Coffey still can be tuned to produce alcohol at near its limit of purity. For chemical reasons, alcohol cannot be produced reliably above 95.57 percent. (Some of you may notice that this is just above the alcohol content of Everclear, a bottled beverage alcohol that's not legal in some states in the United States. If you ever wondered why Everclear "only" went to 190° proof, now you know.)

You might be thinking, "That's not whiskey." And you'd be right, but only by a notch or two. We've briefly mentioned grain whisky, the high-proof distillate that gets aged in wood and (mostly) goes into blended whisky. This is where it comes from, though the still is tuned just a bit lower, and the proof is around 180° (90 percent). I can attest that you actually can smell different grains in something that high in proof. What's more, aged grain whisky can be phenomenal. I'd happily drink J. P. Wiser's 18 year old all afternoon; I have, and it's just a mellow beauty. We'll talk more about grain whisky in chapter 12.

 Wiser's 18

Derisively called "brown vodka," grain whisky can be quite alluring. This delivers soft pencil shavings, vanilla, and butter creams. Smooth waves of sweet caramel and toffee on the tongue, with shivers of oak and cedar. Warm and friendly.

The columns, the beer stills that they run in Kentucky and Canada (not the grain whisky columns) are simpler. As I said, they're very similar to the analyzer column of a Coffey still, and they run to a lower proof. By regulation, as noted earlier, American whiskeys cannot be more than 160° proof (80 percent ABV) coming off the final distillation. To the best of my knowledge, all the major bourbon makers use a second distillation (in either a doubler or a thumper), so the proof coming off the beer still is in the 120° to 140° (60 to 70 precent ABV) area.

Here's how things work in a beer still. The column is of variable diameter; I've seen them as small as 12 inches (30.5 cm), and Buffalo Trace Distillery runs an 84-inch (2 m) monster, the biggest in the bourbon business. (The one at the J. P. Wiser distillery in Windsor, Ontario, is even larger, and puts out distillate at an amazing 240 gallons (908.5 liters) a minute, more than a full-sized fire hose.) They run from about 30 feet (9.1 m) tall to more than 60 feet (18.3 m), but they're all straight columns— no balls, bends; or even squat, fat columns. These aren't pot stills; they're pretty uniform in shape.

In columns, it's about what's *inside*. You have plates, or trays, each one the same diameter as the still. Depending on what the still is for, and how big it is, they may have anywhere from fifteen to more than seventy of these

trays. The trays are perforated with holes; the size varies, but the largest would pass a large man's finger. Then to one side of the tray, alternating sides as you go down through the column, is a wider pipe, with a low dyke around it. This is called the "down-comer."

How it works is pretty simple: The unfiltered beer, mash and all, may start with a run through a beer preheater above the still; it's a kind of protocondenser that uses the hot vapor to heat the beer and cool the vapor. Heated or not, the beer enters the column about three-quarters of the way up and flows downward. As it descends, it fills each tray up to the level of the dyke around the down-comer opening.

Meanwhile, pressurized steam is fed into the bottom of the column. The hot steam rises through the holes in the plates, bubbling through the beer, heating it, and "stripping" the alcohol out of it and carrying it up the column. (That reminds me, these stills are also known as "strippers"; I swear, almost everything in bourbon distillation has at least two names.) As the beer falls, it gets hotter; as the steam rises, it gets cooler. The whole column is pretty hot, though, and the alcohol and congeners continue to rise.

Other, Older Stills

There may be a lot of new distillers using hybrid pot stills with a column and straight-up pot stills to make American-style whiskeys like rye and bourbon (there are a small number using column stills, too). The bulk of bourbon and rye (and corn and wheat) whiskey in America is still made on beer stills, with doublers or thumpers.

The column still didn't always rule American whiskey making. There were other options, not limited to pot stills, though there were some pretty large pot stills making whiskey even post-Prohibition.

Back in the 1800s, there were stills made of wood, and there were reflux columns filled with smooth river rocks. As long as there was copper somewhere in the system—and there always was, usually in the condenser—the design of the still could take various forms, and often, in this time, large wooden beams were cheap and plentiful. They were effective and cheap to repair. When copper became cheaper and rail transport made shipping easier, the wooden stills and the "box of rocks" would fade in favor of more efficient equipment.

However, there was one type of still that's recently gained some new attention: the three-chamber still. It was widely used in rye whiskey distillation even after Prohibition. Rye whiskey historian David Wondrich described it as "a sort of

bolt-action rifle to the pot still's muzzle loader and the column still's machine gun."

What did it look like? Well it was as likely to be made from wood as from copper, even in the late 1800s. It would be a tall cylinder, divided into three chambers by internal barriers. The beer was poured in the top, and low-pressure steam came in from the bottom. The steam rose slowly through the beer in each chamber to the top through copper heat exchangers. The beer would be "cooked" in each chamber for about twenty minutes, compared to the ninety seconds it takes for beer to drop through a Kentucky beer still. As the beer got hotter, it would slowly give up its alcohol, which would rise to the top through valves and pipes and be directed to a doubler, while the spent beer was released through the bottom.

Distillers apparently moved to column stills in the late 1800s but then mostly changed back to the three-chamber still after ten or fifteen years.

The flavor of the distillate was not the same; it was missing a depth, a richness, a character some referred to as a "darkness."

Very few three-chamber stills continued post-Prohibition, and like pot stills, they disappeared in the 1950s. But renewed interest in this throwback type of still has led at least one distiller, Leopold Bros. of Denver, to have one made. We're all waiting to see what the whiskey can do.

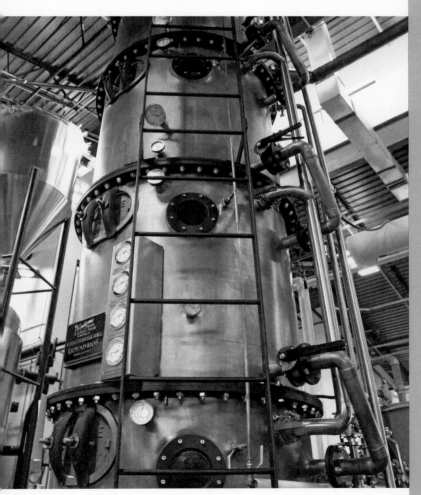

OTHER, OLDER STILLS

New Riff Bourbon

New Riff does bourbon old school on a beer still. Stone-cold classic bourbon nose: cinnamon, hot corn, and slab-cut oak. Amp it up and lay it on the tongue: focused, in the groove, nothing that isn't needed for bourbon.

Jay Erisman, the guy who runs the pot still (and handles strategic development) at New Riff Distilling in Covington, Kentucky, is, perhaps surprisingly, a column still chauvinist. He pointed out that it's not just "beer" that is falling through the column.

"What goes in a Kentucky beer still is all the grains—everything— and those grains get pounded by live steam," he said. "They enter about three-quarters of the way up the still, and on the way down, they're giving up flavor. The beer still allows for that, and that's important for making the biggest, fattest whiskey possible." That grain also becomes "stillage," the future sour mash we talked about in chapter 4.

Once the beer's fallen and the vapors rise above the level of the beer entrance, the upper trays often have something called "bubble caps." That's a copper cap, looking something like a straight-sided mushroom cap or umbrella with slits cut in the lower sides, that fits over each hole in the tray.

As reflux causes the vapor to condense in the upper spaces of the column, the liquid falls through the down-comers and fills the trays. The bubble cap is covered by the liquid, and as vapor comes up through the hole, it bubbles through the slits. The bubble cap keeps distillation going at a steady rate, despite levels of liquid on the trays; it also increases contact with copper, with the resulting cleaning effect on the spirit.

The vapor experiences reflux in the top of the column, falling back, encountering the copper (in the bubble caps and often the entire shell of the column), and eventually escaping. At this point, it either goes to a condenser, and then to the doubler, or it goes directly to the thumper.

The doubler, as explained in the previous chapter, is essentially a continuous pot still. The vapors off the beer still go through a condenser (where they encounter more copper), then, as low wines, go to a reservoir to be fed into the doubler. They are heated in the doubler, and more water and undesirable elements are left behind as the vapors come off and go to a second condenser for the high wines.

A thumper does roughly the same thing, only the vapors don't go through the condenser first; they go directly into the thumper and exit under the liquid in the thumper. This condenses the vapors, heats the liquid, and causes a secondary distillation that cleans and concentrates the alcohol in the distillate.

By the way, in doing the research for this book, I finally got an answer to a question that's been bothering me for years and something you may be wondering, as well. In a pot still, you cut off the heads and tails, and while you redistill them, eventually there's stuff you get rid of. Where does that happen in a beer still?

Dr. Pat Heist, cofounder of Wilderness Trail Distillery in Danville, Kentucky, had the simple answer: "The heads come off [before] the condenser as vapor," he said. "The tails either go into the stillage or they stay in the doubler." The doubler gets emptied and cleaned whenever the column still is shut down for cleaning. There's that question answered.

The distillate is pumped to a spirit well (a simple holding tank) and then to a barrel-filling station; next stop, the warehouse.

BUFFALO TRACE
Doubler Still
Capacity
9,840 gallons

Tuning the Still

You get different distillate from a pot still by design, as we discussed in the previous chapter. But that's then set. You can vary the distillate to a degree by how hard you boil the wash, even by how much wash or low wines you put in, which will leave more bare copper to interact with the spirit vapors.

How do you "tune" a beer still? Jimmy Russell, the legendary master distiller at Wild Turkey Distilling Company, told me how stillmen used to prop a chair up so they could sit, balanced on the chair's back two legs, with their feet up against the column. "You run the still by the sound, the whistle," he said.

The stillman would have one hand on the steam valve and one hand on the beer flow regulator. Some of them, he told me, would doze over the night shift yet be so attuned to the rumble and wash of the still and the whistle that they'd be adjusting it, practically in their sleep—a bit more cold beer to bring the temperature down, a bit more steam to bring it up.

Do I believe him? Russell told the story with a straight face, and he's certainly been around long enough to have seen something like that in a pre-safety-conscious industry. But I don't know that I'd want to play poker with the man.

Still that is how you fiddle with a Kentucky beer still. Adjust the heat with the steam or beer flow, and you get a different distillation, a bit more or less congeners of different types. Stay awake, though.

TUNING THE STILL

Column Complexity

Now that I've explained how the two main types of column stills work and how they differ, we need to talk about the role they play in flavor development. It's been my experience that there's very little agreement on this. Some of that may well stem from the bifurcated vision about column stills and beer stills that I mentioned back at the beginning of the chapter.

Distillers who run pot stills take it as given that pot stills conserve more of the flavor of the wash, the delicate aromas of fermentation, the cereal flavors of the grain. Distillers who run beer stills dispute this vehemently, pointing to the relatively low exit proofs as evidence that there's plenty of "room" for flavor in their distillate. Distillers who are making grain whiskey on Coffey stills don't generally get involved in these arguments; they just keep their still running, filling barrels, and keeping it all consistent. (There are exceptions, like the luscious distillate that comes off Coffey stills at Nikka, and at the Crown Royal distillery in Manitoba.)

When I set out to write this book, I had a grand theory of whiskey making that I'd been working on for a few years, based on conversations with distillers in Scotland, Ireland, and America. It went like this: Single malt whiskeys all use roughly the same yeast, malt, and variety of barrels; and the warehouses in Scotland and Ireland fell into two general categories: the old dunnage warehouses and modern racked ones. The variety in single malts, therefore, came largely from the casks that were used, the amount of peating that was done to the malt, and the type of pot stills and how they were run. The image I had was of a narrow set of choices at the beginning and end of the process, with a broad variance in the distillation step.

For column-distilled bourbon and American-style rye, on the other hand, the image was reversed. My theory was that while the mashbill, yeast, and fermentation regimens were quite varied, and the new barrels could be charred and toasted in different ways and placed in wildly different spots in the warehouses, the beer stills were almost all the same, varying only in diameter. They were a consistent uniformity in the process, with everyone's whiskey coming through there the same. It was not so much flavor creation as uniform flavor conservation.

I was generalizing, of course; but I realized that and accepted that there would be exceptions. But the first time I took it out and showed it to someone—Brown-Forman master distiller Chris Morris— the beer still side got shredded! Morris would be the right man for the job. He's one of the few people responsible for running several large beer stills (at their Louisville plants) *and* big pot stills (at Woodford Reserve) for making whiskey.

"They're uniform in their concept," he said about the beer stills. "But in the world of Brown-Forman, you have diameter as a difference, height, number of plates, copper versus steel versus a combination, steam pressure, heat (they run at different ranges of temperatures), how many trays at the top without beer, how much reflux, and the beer itself: flow rate, water/grain ratio. At the Old Forester distillery, you have the Old Forester recipe

and Early Times recipe, and [along] with all the [other] differences, you also have a difference in distillation proof. You have to make adjustments to how you run that still to get that difference."

He then pointed out that with Woodford Reserve, they do have differences going into the pot still. They don't just make bourbon there but are constantly experimenting with different mashes: rye, malt, and oats, for instance. The wash still is run differently for each of those. "You have to run the spirit safe differently because the cuts are different, because the grain bill is different, and flavor is different," he wound up, "and off we go again."

There are a lot of differences, a lot of options in building and running a beer still, maybe more than most pot still distillers realize. Columns look very industrial, especially to the uninformed eye. That's why I'm thrilled to see the gleaming copper beer still at the new exhibition Brown-Forman has built on Main Street in Louisville. It looks, as I've remarked on social media, like some machine god from *Metropolis*, brilliantly central, posed for pictures. Maybe now beer stills, column stills, will gain some well-deserved respect. Instead of being hidden away, the beer still has taken center stage, wreathed in steam and roaring with power.

A beer still at Wilderness Trail Distillery (Danville, KY)

The Hybrid

There's another type of "column" still that's become quite numerous in craft distilling, and I should explain it. If you've been to a new, small distillery in America or Europe, chances are very good that you've seen one and you may have thought, "Hey, that's a column . . . is that a column still?" You almost certainly didn't see a column still. As far as I know, no one new is running a straight-up Coffey still, and I think I can still count the number of beer stills at "craft" distilleries on the fingers of both hands.

But you very likely saw a hybrid still, or what some call a "pot and column" still. It had something that looked like a column, either sitting right on top of a pot still or maybe off to the side of a pot still, connected to it by piping of various sizes. It probably didn't look big enough to be a column still—not enough ports, not enough plates, and lots of extra levers on it.

The hybrid stills grew out of the stills used for making eau-de-vie and schnapps in Europe, and the biggest maker is the CARL company (we talked about them back in the first distillation chapter). It's not quite a pot still, and it certainly isn't a column still, either.

Mountain Laurel Spirits, the folks in Bristol, Pennsylvania, who make Dad's Hat rye whiskey, are very close to my house; and I stop in fairly often. They have a hybrid still, and cofounder Herman Mihalich was good enough to take me through how it works.

It is a batch process, like a pot still. You fill it with wash (or beer; the stripping run for Dad's Hat is done with the grains in) or low wines and start to cook it. As the vapors start to rise, you'll start a heads cut, then switch over to collecting the hearts when it reaches the right point, the clean point. You'll run that as long as you can, getting clean spirit, then do a tails cut.

Mihalich noted that when he's distilling for aging in their smaller 15-gallon (56.8 liters) barrels, he'll take a sharper, tighter set of cuts. He goes less tight on the distillate destined for the full-sized 53-gallon (200.6 liters) barrels. "We let some of the funk in," as he put it, noting that "the funk becomes flavor in the big barrels."

What about those columns? The columns are there to create reflux opportunities. The viewports and levers on the side are to operate the rectifying plates in the column. The plates start out open. As the operator moves them closed— sort of like a damper on a fireplace, not actually closing the vapor path but restricting it—it slows down the vapor's upward progress, creating reflux.

The column may also have what's called a dephlegmator, which is a kind of internal version of the water jackets on some pot stills or maybe an in-still partial condenser. The dephlegmator sits at the top of the column. It is a series of tubes with water of varying temperature running through them. The temperature varies with how much reflux the operator wants to create.

The hybrid is designed to give the distiller more options to control the distillate. To some extent, it allows the distiller to make more than one pot still out of the pot still. An operator can control the distillation—what regional style it is, how clean it is,

how much *flavor* is in it—by a few methods that can vary different processes in the pot and in the column.

For example, the distiller can increase the steam heat on the pot. More heat means a more energetic separation of vapors and liquid, and an increased carryover of congeners to the distillate, which gives a fatter, heavier spirit some funk in it, like Mihalich said. Shut down the dephlegmator and open the plates and you increase the effect. Increase the flow of water to the dephlegmator to lower its temperature and you'll make it rain in there: lots of reflux, a much cleaner spirit making it out of the still, and more of the lighter flavors becoming evident. The question is: What kind of whiskey do you want to make? You have options.

That's the whole idea of a hybrid still: to give the operator more options, to put several stills into one. You can open everything wide and make a fat, wobbly whiskey, or screw it down and chill it, and make lighter whiskey. You can add a rectifying column and really crank it down to make vodka. You can even put a gin head on it, a big bulgy copper cap with no outlets, pour grain neutral spirits (more about these in chapter 12) and botanicals into the pot, and just redistill in place till you have the flavor you want.

Dad's Hat Bonded

Dad's Hat is rye made in a hybrid still. That's righteous rye, dry grain with a hint of dill and mint. Flavors roll around: that rye grain, sweet malt, wood-spice, just a rim of dill, and a long finish. Plenty going on.

That's one reason small distilleries buy the hybrid still: more options, more ways to make spirits, because a lot of small distilleries have to make vodka and gin (and aquavit!) to generate cash flow. They want to be able to experiment with different types of distillate for whiskey because they need to find the right setup for the whiskey that becomes theirs.

The other reason for a hybrid still is because running a column still, a Coffey or beer still, is an undertaking. The idea of a continuous still is to reach efficiencies by making a lot of spirit. If you aren't selling a lot of spirit, if you don't have the capital to buy enough barrels and storage space to take up the output of a column still, then you probably don't want to take that on until you're ready.

No matter what still you have, to get whiskey out of the distillate you just made, you have to put it in barrels. That's next.

A hybrid still and distillers John Cooper and Herman Mihalich making Dad's Hat Pennsylvania Rye Whiskey

The Barrel

I find it fascinating to recall that when I first became seriously interested in whiskey, more than twenty years ago, the majority of whiskey drinkers didn't give the barrel a second thought. They were blissfully unaware of the enormous contributions of the barrel to the whiskey and often didn't even realize that every bit of color in whiskey comes from the barrel.

Now, twenty-odd years further on, everyone can quote you the rule of thumb that 50 percent (or 60 percent, or 70 percent, depending on whose thumb it is) of whiskey's flavor comes from the barrel. They may even know that there's a difference in the contribution of new, charred barrels, toasted barrels, or used sherry casks; and they'll be quick to tell you that the majority of flavor comes from the barrel.

That's *the* main reason I wrote the book: to point out what I quoted renowned Scotch whisky blender Dr. Bill Lumsden saying back in the very first chapter. It's worth quoting him again. "If the barrel gives a whisky 50 percent of its flavor," he said, "that just means that the other 50 percent *doesn't* come from the barrel."

We're going to talk about the barrel in this chapter, but remember that the barrel needs all the flavors that come from each of the processes before it to work with. Because otherwise you've wasted your mash and fermentation, and you'll get what folks derisively refer to as "brown vodka," whiskey that's been stripped down too far before entering the wood, so that all it comes out with is color and a faint taste of a lumberyard. The flavor of a good whiskey is the effect of the synergy of combining the flavors of the new make and the flavors of the barrel, along with the physical changes of maturation, developing something that's much more than either of them alone.

King Oak

Whenever we talk about whiskey barrels, assume that they are made of oak unless they are specifically identified as being made of another wood.

The regulations for making Scotch whisky and American whiskey are clear: They must be aged in oak. Almost every other whiskey is also aged in oak for a few very good reasons. First those American whiskeys are almost all using brand new oak barrels, only once. The used barrels are plentiful and relatively cheap, so they're popular. Sherry casks are oak, as are the other wine barrels most commonly used for aging whiskey: port, Madeira, and various reds.

But the main reason oak is used, and the reason the regulations in Scotland and America require it, is because it works really well. Oak has a lot to recommend it, several species in particular.

First of all, oak is just waterproof enough. There are structures at the cellular level in oak that are called *tyloses*, that are essentially small plugs that develop in the channels that pass liquid, sugar, and nutrients through the living wood, the sapwood. As the tree grows and gains more of the woody outer layers, tyloses will block the channels, protecting the live wood of the tree from losses in times of drought, or if the tree is infected.

The tyloses will not pass liquids. But they will pass air and other gases, like alcohol and water in vapor form, as the liquids more slowly seep through the interstitial spaces in the wood. This is the source of the slow evaporative loss that's known as the "angel's share," a loss that can run as high as 10 percent a year in hot climates or as low as 1 percent in the wet, cold climate of northern Scotland.

More importantly for flavor development, oak is simply stuffed full of delicious flavors. The processes involved in making barrels out of trees don't just make barrels; they create even more flavor compounds.

Is it all a happy accident, much like the ideal nature of copper for stills? Or did whiskey makers evolve to using oak, to charring it, to toasting it? I think we can put the use of oak down largely to its waterproof nature. But charring was used for its effects on color and flavor, and toasting was discovered by winemakers and adapted to use in aging whiskey. Oak is a gifted wood, and the various species used for whiskey all contribute different flavors to the process.

I wanted to get smarter about whiskey wood, so I talked to Stuart MacPherson, the Spanish operations manager for the Edrington Group, the company that owns The Macallan, The Glenrothes, and Highland Park distilleries. His title reflects the importance of sherry casks for those whiskies; his former title was master of wood for The Macallan.

What MacPherson told me was influenced by their latest research on the flavor effects of wood on whiskey, and it's startling stuff. "People are beginning to understand that the biggest influence in any liquid is down to the individual wood species, or the preparation," he said. "They'd talk about this spirit or the previous use, but fundamentally, it's very much driven by the wood and the process. The new make spirit goes into the barrel, and it's which species [of] oak it is and what toasting regimen was used that will have the biggest influence."

In other words, the base wood of a barrel continues to have greater effect in future aging or finishing than whatever wine or spirit it may have previously held. That's going to blow some minds—it already has and created controversy— but with that in mind, let's take a look at the different species before getting into making and filling barrels.

Barrels awaiting recoopering at Speyside Cooperage, in Scotland.

Quercus alba: White Oak

White oak from the forests of Missouri and Arkansas makes up the lion's share of bourbon barrels. It grows relatively straight and clean, with few branches in the first 20 feet (6.1 m). The cellular structure is fairly loose, but with the effect of the tyloses and the quarter-sawing technique that cuts across the growth rings to take the most advantage of that effect, white oak will make a watertight barrel.

White oak, once air-dried, toasted, and charred, will yield a distinct set of flavors to a whiskey. This species has more vanilla, citrus, and coconut sources than in the other species favored for barrels. The barrels are charred for use in aging bourbon, and that char will also act as a filter for the sulfur compounds found in corn.

Quercus alba: Pedunculate Oak

Q. robur is also known as Limousin, or French oak, because of the large forests of *Q. robur* that grow in the Limousin area of France. It also grows in Eastern Europe, often mingled with *Q. petraea*. The largest part of the harvest of *Q. robur* goes to the wine industry,

but it is also used in barrels for cognac and Armagnac, and for sherry, port, and Madeira, the fortified wines whose *Q. robur* casks are prized for whiskey aging. *Q. robur* is less dense than white oak, but has a tighter grain and higher levels of tannins. The grain makes it necessary to split the oak rather than sawing it to get a watertight barrel.

Whiskey will get flavors of dried fruits, spice, leather, and chocolate from *Q. robur*.

Quercus petraea: Sessile Oak

Q. petraea is what most people are thinking of when they talk about Hungarian oak, for the same reason that *Q. robur* is thought of as Limousin oak; there are extensive forests in Hungary of almost all *Q. petraea*. It is just beginning to be used for whiskey making and has lower levels of tannins than *Q. robur* but is described as "quite aromatic" by winemakers.

Quercus garryana: Oregon Oak

Q. garryana grows on the West Coast of the United States in an area much smaller than it used to. It is largely protected now, so coopers are making barrels from trees that are either newly harvested from private lands or that had already been cut or fallen. The high level of tannins requires extra-long air drying to leach the astringency out of the wood. Once that's done, *Q. garryana* will give aromas of dark fruit and tangy smoke, almost like a sweet Kansas City barbecue sauce. Westland Distillery in Seattle has been doing some groundbreaking work with *Q. garryana* aging.

Japanese-grown mizunara represents a tiny portion of whiskey barrels overall, but the interest in the whiskey aged in them has been intense. These trees take two to five times as long to reach barrel-making maturity. Not only do they have to be tall enough; their porous wood requires a larger-diameter trunk to be cut in a way that prevents too much leakage.

Mizunara gives aromas of sandalwood and spice. Like *Q. garryana*, it is only used in a small handful of whiskies.

 Westland Garryana

American single malt, aged in Garryana oak. A big sweet/acid edge, like a Kansas City barbecue sauce. Roars on the palate but doesn't blow out the sweet malt or the cocoa notes. Dynamic balance of two huge influences.

Quercus mongolica: Mizunara Oak

 Yama Mizunara

Bainbridge Organic Distillers paid dearly for some *mizunara* barrels to age their unmalted barley spirit. It yields aromas of sandalwood, tropical fruit (ripe firm mango), putty, and spicy oak, and bright flavors of ripe fruit, busy woodshop, vanilla, and allspice. Money well spent.

Quercus rubra: Northern Red Oak

I only include *Q. rubra* here because I was at the J. P. Wiser distillery, in Windsor, Ontario, and their master blender, Dr. Don Livermore, let me try a sample of a whisky he was aging in red oak as an experiment. Red oak leaks a lot and has a very strong flavor of wet, raw wood that I didn't find particularly pleasant. "What are you going to do with *that*," I asked, and he patiently answered, "Blend it," reminding me once again that he makes Canadian whisky, which is blended. Still I saw him a few years later, and he told me that a group of bartenders were agitating for him to bottle it unblended. Truly there is no accounting for taste.

Making Barrels Creates Flavor

Oak is an aromatic wood. If you've ever been at a cutting site and smelled the tangy wetness of fresh-cut oak, you know there's a lot to work with.

Flavor is already *in* the oak when it's about to be cut to make barrels. But the full process of bringing oak from the forest to the point of filling a finished barrel with new make spirit refines those flavors and aromas and creates new ones. Here's how it works:

(Keep in mind that we're talking mainly about bourbon barrels here, at first, since that's the vast majority of whiskey that uses new barrels. We'll get to refills later.)

Sawyers are the first folks in the chain, the people who go out in the woods with chainsaws. They're usually cutting for general lumber, but they are always looking for oaks that are the right size for making barrels because those trees are worth more money. The diameter will vary with the type of oak, but it's somewhere between 14 inches (35.6 cm) and 27 inches (68.6 cm). They need to be able to get at least one 4 foot (1.2 m)-tall set of staves out of the log, preferably two, before hitting the first branch.

Branches mean knots; knots mean leaks.

Flavor creation begins when the logs arrive at the mill yard. They will be kept wet until they're ready to be cut into staves. As the logs sit wet, constantly hosed down by water guns, tannins begin to leach out of the wood. You can see the darkness in the runoff. Beneficial fungus has begun growing on the wood that's doing similar things: breaking down tannins and also making sugars out of cellulose.

When it's their turn, the logs will be cut into staves, which are still flat at this point; the curving comes later. Then they'll be stacked in a drying yard for seasoning. It seems counterintuitive to see open-air drying yards where the wood gets soaked by every passing shower, but it's not the wood's surface that's being dried. Water is coming out of the wood's dead cells, and as it does, it brings more tannins with it.

The wood is seasoned to the liking of the individual distilleries: some as short as three months, some as long as twenty-four months or even longer. Then it is usually kilned to get the moisture level uniform so every stave behaves the same when being shaped.

The staves go from there to the cooperage to be made into barrels. The moisture level may be uniform, but by this time—unless something notably unusual has been going on—the staves cut from a given tree are scattered throughout the yard, and it's unlikely that they'll wind up in the same barrel. Call it uniformity through chaos, as each barrel has a random assortment of trees represented in its staves.

The staves are cut to uniform lengths and shaped with one side (the outer side) slightly wider so they will fit together in circular barrel form. Widths are inevitably *not* similar, due to the pattern of quarter-sawn logs. Then the coopers pull staves and place them in a circular jig, "raising" the barrels, and achieving remarkably similar dimensions, working only by eye to judge the size of the staves that will go together. It takes them about a minute, and it's fascinating to watch.

Now the staves are briefly steamed to make the wood pliable, and the two ends are drawn together by tightening a cable around them, creating a tight seal. This also begins flavor creation again, incredibly. The lignin in the oak, the "woody" part that gives it strength and structure, has been breaking down into sugars and vanillin (which tastes exactly the way you'd think it does—it's used in artificial vanilla flavoring) during the seasoning, and this physical stress of bending continues that process. The next step will accelerate it.

Heat comes next, either a slow, radiant heat for what's called "toasting," or a roaring direct flame that will actually char the wood to a varying degree, depending on the distiller's specifications. The heat changes the oak, physically and chemically, making a wooden container into a chemical-reaction chamber, a filter, and an infusion vessel.

Depending on who the cooperage is making the barrel for, the first step may be to toast the wood. This involves heating it with an electric element or, more traditionally, by placing the still open-ended barrel over a small fire of wood chips. Toasting changes the sugar makeup of the wood surfaces and caramelizes other sugars. Not every distiller requests toasting.

Toasted or not, a bourbon barrel is then charred. This high-intensity treatment with an open gas flame literally chars the inside of the barrel, creating caramels, breaking down more lignin to create more sugars and vanillin. These are concentrated in a layer just below the char, a reddish layer that's simply called the "red layer."

Something Unusual: Buffalo Trace's Single Oak Project

Back in 1999, the folks at Buffalo Trace Distillery in Frankfort, Kentucky, started an ambitious project that had something quite unusual at its core. Working with barrel maker Independent Stave Company (ISC, the world's largest maker of whiskey and wine barrels), they arranged for ninety-six oaks to be cut and carefully kept track of each stave cut from the top and bottom of each log.

After seasoning, the staves from each top and each bottom were put together by ISC's coopers; each top making one barrel, each bottom making one barrel, 192 barrels in all.

Seven different factors were varied: mashbill (wheat or rye bourbon), entry proof (105° or 125° proof), stave seasoning (six or twelve months), wood grain size (tight, average, or coarse), warehouse type (concrete or wooden floor), barrel char level (three or four), and the big one: tree cut, whether the wood for the barrel came from the top or bottom half of the harvested log. The "top" is just the top of that bottom log of the tree, what they call the "money log." Anything above that is usually cut for railroad ties or pallets, at a much lower rate paid to the sawyer.

The filled barrels were aged for eight years, then bottled with numbers that were tagged to the different variables, known only to the distillery at that time. They were released on the market, and customers were encouraged to enter their opinions of the various bottles online.

Buffalo Trace gathered this crowd-sourced data and threw it into a huge spreadsheet. There were about a dozen that rose to the top, but the ultimate favorite was a rye recipe bourbon, entered at 125° proof into a barrel charred to a number four depth, made from staves cut from the bottom half of a tree with average grain and air-seasoned for twelve months, and aged for eight years in a concrete-floored warehouse.

But the real lesson of the exercise, according to Buffalo Trace master distiller Harlen Wheatley, was that making good whiskey actually depended on mixing things up—that "uniformity through chaos" I mentioned. "We realized that our regular bourbons need to have barrels made from randomly sourced logs," Wheatley said, "not all bottoms or tops, not all from one place. They all have something to offer." Besides, as Buffalo Trace president Mark Brown pointed out, it's not like they could go through the forest only cutting down the bottom of trees.

The char itself is a highly effective filter that will pull undesirable flavors out of the spirit. Char level is measured on a 1 to 7 scale that rises with depth of char; most whiskey barrels are between a 3 and a 4.

The heads of the barrels are now fitted. The heads have also been either toasted or charred; some distillers choose to only toast the heads without charring them, exposing the spirit to a greater amount of the toasted sugars and caramels.

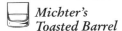

Michter's Toasted Barrel

Finished in toasted (not charred) barrels. Vanilla and horchata with spikes of oak fill the rich nose. Some heat on the palate, but gentle waves of vanilla and light spice soothe it sweetly. Lovely stuff.

The barrel is done, at least as far as flavor-creating work is concerned. A bunghole is drilled and a bung fitted, then water is poured into it and the barrel is plugged and pressurized to check for leaks. Any leaks are repaired with a fascinating selection of special tools, small wedges and plugs of wood, and reeds (which are thin enough to slip into a crack, and then swell to seal it). Once it's watertight, the barrel is shipped.

The wine barrels destined for refill as whiskey barrels are built in largely the same manner, though in different sizes and shapes, and the European oak is not quarter-sawn but split. The barrels are usually toasted but will not be charred.

Hooping new barrels at Brown-Forman Cooperage (Louisville, KY) (top); Barrelheads getting charred (below)

Bungs: The Other Wood

Whiskey barrels are filled through a bunghole, which is plugged with a wooden bung. The bung is often made of poplar, not oak. Some distillers do use oak; Maker's Mark uses walnut. But the great majority use poplar.

Why poplar? It's cheap and plentiful, it's soft (but not too soft), and it expands well to make a tight seal. The important question is whether it has any influence on the flavor of the whiskey. It doesn't, but not because it's poplar. If the warehouse workers have done their jobs right, the bung is on the topmost stave as the barrel rests through the years. They're placed that way to minimize leaks. The bung isn't actually touching the whiskey, so no flavor. Simple.

A selection of bungs, wedges, and spiles

Entry Proof

"Entry proof" is the alcohol proof at which the new make goes into the barrel. The legal maximum for American whiskey is 125° proof.

A distillery would be tempted to put the whiskey in at higher proof because it's cheaper. You can fit more higher-proof whiskey into fewer barrels, and barrels cost money, as does warehouse space to age them. But the higher entry proof isn't traditional, and some distillers have decided that lower entry proof makes their whiskey taste better, even though it's more expensive to do so.

For some distillers, that's worth the money. For some, it's not the preferred character of their whiskey when it's done that way. Is it better at lower entry proof? Some people think so, but recall the results of the blind crowd-sourced tasting for the Buffalo Trace Single Oak Project: People preferred a whiskey that had a high entry proof. Like a lot of things with whiskey, low entry proof isn't better or worse; it's another choice.

Palletized Barrels

A barrel has traditionally had the filling hole in the side, in one of the wider staves. Since this hole, no matter how tightly bunged (the plug is known as a "bung," and the hole therefore is a "bunghole," making the stave the "bung stave"), is the spot most likely to leak, it is part of the warehouse crew's job to "clock" the barrels as they roll them into the racks. That means they're placing them so that when the barrel comes to rest, the bung is on the top stave and won't leak.

Through experience, they know where to place the bung stave as they roll each barrel in; that changes with each barrel rolled into the rack.

Some distillers have begun to place their barrels on end, on pallets. The bung is in one of the heads. Once the barrels are filled, they're strapped together—usually four to a pallet—and the pallet is then put in place in the warehouse by forklift. A very expensive, sparkless forklift.

These palletized warehouses can hold a much greater density of barrels, as they can be stacked with only the strength of the barrel and the pallet to hold them up. The barrels are easier to move and place than with muscle power. The downside is that they are harder to pull apart to get at particular barrels, and there isn't as much air circulation. There also is not as much contact with the wood on the heads of the barrels—exactly half as much. If you want to toast your heads rather than char them, this is an issue.

Palletization remains the choice of the individual distiller. It also can make for good whiskey.

Filling the Barrels

We'll cover more of this in the chapter on aging, but let's talk about what's going to be delivered (and taken away) from the whiskey pretty quickly in the first few years of interaction with the barrel. As has been said several times, the barrel delivers the largest part of the flavor to a whiskey. But it's relatively easy to explain because it is so concentrated and so direct. There are flavors in the oak; alcohol and water pull them out.

When the barrel arrives at the distillery for its first filling, it is almost always an American distillery. The strong flavors a new barrel will impart are generally considered overpowering to other types of whiskey (though, as mentioned above, there are a few exceptions to this rule, and other makers continue to experiment with them).

Whenever I think about what goes on in a new, charred oak barrel as new make becomes whiskey, a Winston Churchill quote comes to mind. The politician, author, and adventurer was noted as having said, "I have taken more out of alcohol than alcohol has taken out of me." Whatever he meant by that, aging in a new barrel is partly a question of absorption running in two ways.

It's more about the water than the alcohol. Some of the flavor components in the oak are more soluble in water than alcohol, and they tend to give whiskey a dry, astringent character. When the water pulls them out of the wood, they will oxidize as the slow air exchange takes place in the barrel. More water equals more oxidized astringent compounds, and that means smoother whiskey.

Alcohol and water are both solvents (technically, when they are combined, whichever one is present in higher percentage is a solvent, and the other is a solute, but…). As they penetrate the char and the red layer, they absorb the color, which becomes the color of the whiskey.

They also start pulling out the sugars, vanillin, and other flavors. There are two isomers of oak lactones: cis-lactone gives the whiskey a sweet vanilla-coconut character; trans-lactone yields a spicier blend of cloves and coconut but is weaker. Methyl salicylate is present in low levels in some white oak; it gives a minty aroma to young whiskeys.

Meanwhile, the alcohol is continuing the work of lignin breakdown begun during the air-drying phase (it's a long process), adding more sugars and aldehydes, which will break down into esters, yielding varying levels of fig, tobacco, cinnamon/spice, and smoke aromas. As the alcohol continues to break down other parts of the wood, melanoidins are produced that deepen the flavors and add more color; and other compounds can add aromas of butterscotch, lighter caramels, and nuts.

On the other side of the absorption balance, the char is at work. Charcoal is one of the most effective filters known and has a simply amazing internal structure.

Consider this: A single gram of charcoal has about *2152.8 square feet (200 m²)* of effective surface area that can grab and sequester unwanted aromatic compounds. Any sulfur compounds in the corn that got past the copper in the stills will be grabbed by the char.

The char layer may only be subtracting flavor, not creating it; but that subtractive effect allows additional flavor to be added. Because of the char, distillers don't have to run as tight a cut on distillation, leaving some good flavor behind in the still in the effort of leaving out all the bad. Instead more of both can come over and be left to the char to sort out.

The Lincoln County Process

Is Jack Daniel's (or George Dickel) bourbon? It's a question that raises hackles among American whiskey drinkers.

CASK? BARREL?

It got me thrown out of a bar once. It starts as bourbon, but it also then becomes Tennessee whiskey. Opinion differs on whether that means it is no longer bourbon.

One thing's for sure, though. Up until the moment the spirit goes through what's called the Lincoln County Process, it's most definitely bourbon.

But then it is filtered ("mellowed," the distillery calls it) through a bed of sugar maple charcoal 10 feet (3.5 m) deep (13 feet [4 m] at Dickel).

There are more details—Jack Daniel burns their own charcoal on-site; Dickel chills their charcoal vats—but the basics are plain. Between the final distillation and entry into the barrel, the spirit is filtered through charcoal, before aging.

What difference does this make in terms of flavor creation or flavor change? I've tasted the new make at Dickel after the beer still—sweet, rough, muddled—and after passing through the doubler—it was cleaner, more identifiably a corn spirit. But after the charcoal, it was like a corn eau-de-vie, powerfully pure and focused. Things have been taken out that allow others to shine.

You can argue that's a good thing, that it's cleaner; or that it's a bad thing, that any flavor taken out is flavor lost. But I'll tell you this: It has a real effect, and it's not just a gimmick. I guess that is why that continues to be part of the process for making Tennessee whiskey.

If you still want to argue about whether it's bourbon or not, well, as the bartender told me, you'll have to take it outside. You're not having that argument in my book.

Jack Daniel's Single Barrel

Jack Daniel's Single Barrel filters through a bed of charcoal before barreling. Deeply sweet smoky corn on the nose, with a bit of barrel oak. Big sweet cooked corn flavor, smooth and mellow, with oak heat on the finish.

THE LINCOLN COUNTY PROCESS

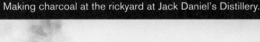

Making charcoal at the rickyard at Jack Daniel's Distillery.

Cask? Barrel?

You'll see the words "barrel" and "cask" used almost interchangeably. Are they actually different? Not really.

Unlike the particular word "hogshead," which means a barrel of between 225 liters (59.4 gallons) and 250 liters (66 gallons)—more below on why)—or the "American standard barrel," which in the bourbon industry is a 53-gallon (200.6 liters) barrel, simply saying barrel or cask means the familiar round container made of oak staves bound by steel hoops. "Cask strength" and "barrel proof" mean the same thing: bottled at the strength the whiskey was when dumped from the cask or from the barrel.

Scots tend to say "cask," and Americans and Canadians tend to say "barrel." But no one's really hard nosed about it—not the way they are about the "correct" way to spell "whiskey" or "whisky." And that's about the same difference.

If that seems like a very brief description of what's going on in the barrel, which we've said several times is the source of 50 percent of the flavor of the whiskey, remember: We've got two more chapters on the flavor creation that takes place in the warehouse and during aging. Here we're only looking at potential.

Now that we've "first-filled" the barrels with bourbon (we'll just take the sherry and port casks as done, because this isn't a sherry flavor-creation book), it's time to look at the important question of what's left for the Scotch, Irish, Canadian, and Japanese distillers to work with.

The folks in the respective industries joke about this. American distillers say that once they've used the barrels once, there's no flavor left in them and the other distillers are welcome to them. The other distillers joke about using bourbon to soak the harsh woodiness out of the barrels to get them to the point where they're good for making "real" whiskey. All in good fun, but at the core, that is what's going on. That first aging does take a lot out of the barrel, and the flavors imparted to the next occupant are more restrained.

First Fills, Ex-Fills, Refills

We need to define our terms on new and used barrels.

New, charred: the classic bourbon barrel; new barrel, new char, will be used once for American whiskey

Ex-bourbon: a used barrel that first aged bourbon

Ex-sherry: a used barrel that first aged sherry

First fill: the first fill with whiskey as a used barrel (technically, it's the second fill)

Second fill, refill: the second fill as a used barrel; some distillers classify any filling after the first one as a "refill" rather than enumerating multiple refills

Virgin bourbon barrel: confusingly, this is a new charred oak barrel that is being used to age other spirits than bourbon; often used as a finishing barrel

Virgin oak: a new barrel, not charred but toasted, used to age spirits that are customarily aged in used barrels; often used as a finishing barrel

Consider, however, the used sherry cask. New make bourbon yanks flavor from the wood with an alcohol percentage that's at least a bit over 50 percent. Sherry, on the other hand, is easing in at around 18 percent ABV. It's not going to be taking as much out of the wood, leaving more for the new make to pull on first refill. This levels out, of course; and by second refill, the two types of cask are about even.

Fill a freshly used bourbon cask with new make—Scotch, Irish, Canadian, Japanese—and you'll be getting an echo of what the bourbon took from the oak: caramel, vanilla, coconut, and smoke, with some light citrus touches. Fill a freshly used sherry cask and you'll get what the European oak has to offer, in greater (leftover) amounts: dried fruit, chocolate, spice.

Now, let's go back to what Stuart MacPherson said at the beginning of the chapter, about how the flavor imparted to new make in first-fill casks is more about the wood than what was in the barrel before. Common wisdom was that when new make was entered into a used cask, much of the flavor and color came from the previous occupant: the bourbon, the rye, the sherry. But from MacPherson's research, it's more that the bourbon gets bourbon-like flavor from the American white oak, the sherry takes flavor from the European oak, and then the new make on the refill does that same thing to a lesser degree. The new make—Scotch, Irish, whatever—is not taking flavor from the leftover bourbon or sherry in some tiny volume, long-duration, mixed-use solera.

The differences among the casks that held the lighter sherries—fino, Manzanilla, even oloroso—will be much smaller, with the flavors largely down to the oak. "For me," said MacPherson, "you'll see a lot more difference in a good PX [Pedro Ximénez] cask, when the sugar content is higher. I think it's more the wines that have a higher sugar content: port, PX, Madeira. The differences are obvious."

As many have said of aging in used barrels, a cask is like a tea bag. The more times you fill it, the less flavor you'll get out of it. Why then, would a distiller want to use anything but first-fill ex-bourbon, first-fill ex-sherry? Because those flavors can be overwhelming and may mask the spirit character altogether. That's when a blender will add in some refill casks, ones that have been used once for bourbon or sherry, then again for a new spirit. Those less heavily flavored casks can be used to create a lighter whiskey, a whiskey more amenable to blending with other flavors, or a whiskey destined for long, long aging.

GlenDronach 15

Aged fifteen years in PX and oloroso sherry casks. Sherry bomb: Rich dried fruits, furniture polish, faint baking spices. All repeated on the tongue, with a good oaky grip on the long finish.

At any point in a used barrel's life, it can be recoopered into a larger barrel. You'll see bourbon hogsheads, larger than any bourbon barrel is, but made to fit Scottish warehouses. The barrels can also be recharred to bring new sugars and caramels to the surface, along with more vanilla, smoke, and the like.

Many distillers have gone to using a barrel for fewer cycles, only refilling once or twice. It costs more, but the flavor is more distinct. Other distillers may use barrels as many as five times, by which point the barrels are weepy with leaks and will likely have to be retired.

That's where the first part of the story of barrels ends. In the next chapter, we'll talk about where the barrels go and what happens to build flavor there. Then we'll return to the barrels for the long, long haul and talk about what happens during the aging process.

Barrels of Clynelish whiskey inside Brora Distillery, Scotland. The distillery closed in 1983 and is currently being refurbished to reopen in 2020.

The Warehouse

Chapter 10:

Barrels do a huge job in giving whiskeys the flavor we cherish. As I told you in the previous chapter, the oak holds a great amount of sugars, vanillin, and other flavors, as well as the important char layer that acts to filter the spirit's less desirable flavors. The influence of the barrel cannot be overstated when it comes to the whiskey in your glass: every bit of color, the lion's share of the flavor.

The barrel can't do all that on its own. It has two necessary allies. The first, which we'll take on in the next chapter, is time. The barrel needs time to create the flavors, to transfer and enrich and transmute the compounds in the wood into the whiskey; time to give up that small percentage of spirit to the air, the so-called "angel's share," that is so important to maturity; time for oxygen to slowly creep through the wood to replace that missing liquid.

But the barrel also needs a place to live. That's the warehouse, and like other whiskey components that influence flavor, they come in a bewildering variety. There are low, one-story warehouses and towering seven-story behemoths that can hold more than 50,000 barrels each. The brick warehouse at Castle & Key in Kentucky, the world's longest whiskey warehouse, is more than 500 feet (152.4 m) long and can hold about 33,000 barrels.

Warehouses can be made out of brick and are also made of stone, concrete, steel, and wood frames skinned in sheet metal. Small distillers may use garages, truck trailers, or shipping containers as warehouses. Some warehouses are heated; most are not and rely on the climate to change the temperatures inside. Barrels may be stacked on dirt floors, they may sit on end atop pallets, and they may be rolled into racks.

Barrels will sit in warehouses for months, years, decades. A very few distillers move the barrels about inside the warehouses, but mostly when a barrel has been placed in a warehouse, it's there till it's time to harvest it. Let's talk about how that affects the flavor of the whiskey.

Dirt and Damp

One of my most enduring memories of whiskey is a visit to The Dalmore. I parked in a gravel lot so close to the Cromarty Firth (an estuary that empties into the Moray Firth, and then the North Sea) that I could have pegged one of the larger rocks into the water.

After a great tour of the distillery (bits of which you've already heard about), we wound up in one of their "dunnage" warehouses.

A dunnage warehouse is very old school. It's low, usually made of brick or stone with a slate roof, and will have a dirt floor, perhaps with wooden ramps for the barrels to roll along. The barrels are stacked on each other, three high. This is how warehouses used to be built in Scotland—everywhere, really, but they survive here—though the growth in the industry led to the adoption of racked, multifloor steel warehouses in the 1950s. Some of the old ones survive.

That Dalmore warehouse was a revelation, a milestone in my whisky education. It was dark, and cool, and damp inside; and when my guide closed the doors, it brought a palpable silence to the thick-walled space. The hard-packed dirt underfoot, the dark-stained barrels lent an air of endless age to the scene that was enhanced by motes of dust drifting through the spears of sunlight spiking down from small holes in the roof.

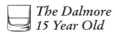 **The Dalmore
15 Year Old**

Can you taste a dunnage warehouse? I smell that stemmy grape; I taste fruit and oak, with a hint of minerality. There's a definite sense of place.

But it wasn't what we saw that made the impression on me that has lasted through years and many other warehouse visits. It was what we smelled. I pulled my notebook from that day: *"aroma in here is unique, SALT, stemmy grape, malt."*

The salt was the briny air blowing off the firth, permeating the warehouse. The malt, obviously, was from the barrels breathing and a bit of spillage. The stemmy grape was off the sherry casks, and it was strong. The whole thing was underlain with the damp smell of the earth itself.

Dunnage warehouse at The Dalmore distillery (Scotland)

That's how dunnage works. The thick walls, slate roof, and dirt floor keep temperature swings at a slow pace. The dampness cuts down on loss, on exchange of vapor. The stacked barrels allow free air circulation. The downside is that moving the barrels is all manual labor, one at a time.

Compare the fairly large Dalmore dunnage to another waterside dunnage warehouse, a much more famous one: Bowmore Distillery's No. 1 Vaults on Islay, dating to the turn of the nineteenth century and believed to be the oldest whisky warehouse anywhere. The stone structure sits on the shore of Loch Indaal, the sea loch that almost cuts Islay in two. It actually sits

behind a wall, partly because the lashing winds across the loch will blast spray across the area and the wall provides some cover, but the main reason is because the floor of the No. 1 Vaults is just below sea level. The wall is a seawall.

 *Bowmore Small Batch*

Aged by the sea in ex-bourbon casks. Enticing mix of vanilla, briny smoke, and soft fruit. Lively on the tongue: The vanilla and smoke go back and forth and wind up on the beach.

(continued on page 156)

Disaster

Sometimes storing whiskey in warehouses can cause complete flavor destruction. Anytime you get thousands of barrels of whiskey together, there's the potential for disaster, if only because huge amounts of whiskey can be affected—or ruined—at one time.

Warehouse-destroying disasters are why warehouses are filled piecemeal, a few days in one, then a week in another, so that, for instance, all the 5-year-old whiskey won't be lost in one night.

Warehouses are vulnerable to structural failure from the sustained weight of the barrels. A full 53-gallon (200.6 liters) bourbon barrel weighs about 500 pounds (about 226.8 kg); thousands of them add up to a huge amount. Loading or unloading the wrong way can stress the racks and lead to collapse, or a warehouse may simply get too old to support the weight. One of the older Barton 1792 distillery warehouses in Bardstown, Kentucky, collapsed in two stages in 2018, spilling thousands of barrels and crushing some.

In 2010, Glenfiddich also suffered a warehouse collapse in Scotland. This one was caused by heavy snows, and the weight of the white stuff eventually stove in the roofs on several warehouses, allowing tons of snow and subzero cold to pour in on the barrels. The distillery

manager saw this as opportunity, though, and pulled the barrels exposed to the extreme cold together to make a blended malt named Snow Phoenix.

Similarly, in 2006, a tornado ripped off part of the roof and brick walls of Warehouse C at Buffalo Trace Distillery in Frankfort, Kentucky. Reconstruction began fairly quickly, but the delicacy of repairing an older building meant that many of the barrels were exposed to the open air for most of the summer. The barrels were blended to create what was known as E. H. Taylor Jr. Warehouse C "Tornado Surviving" bourbon (more about that in a later sidebar).

A few bourbon warehouses have been hit by tornadoes—they're fairly common in Kentucky—and *twisted*. The buildings themselves will be skewed by the power of the cyclonic winds. That seems like an aesthetic problem until you consider that the racks inside are all twisted as well, and now you literally cannot get the barrels out of them. Jim Beam master distiller Fred Noe told me that they tried untwisting one of their tornado-hit warehouses, setting up huge bollards and attaching cables to the warehouses from powerful winches. "But we couldn't get it straight," he said. "You wind up just breaking it up and getting out as many barrels as you can."

The worst disaster that can befall a warehouse is fire. There have been several warehouse fires in Kentucky over the past few decades, and they are roaring. Imagine 5,000-odd tons (4500-ish metric tons) of seasoned oak and 60-plus percent alcohol catching fire. Barrels explode and fly through the air; the heat is felt hundreds of feet away.

The worst in living memory was the 1996 fire at Heaven Hill in Bardstown. About 90,000 barrels were lost, as well as the distillery itself. The flames could be seen 30 miles (48.3 km) away, and a river of fire more than a foot (0.3 m) deep rolled down the hill at one point. When it was all over, the distillery was a concrete slab with melted metal drooped all over it. The warehouses… well, they were just heaps of steel hoops. Everything else burned or melted. Heaven Hill rebuilt, and the industry learned a new set of rules that included sprinklers to stop fires and berms around warehouses to contain burning liquid.

Then there's creeling. I saw a plumb bob in a Heaven Hill warehouse once, just inside the door. There was a chalked circle about 4 feet (1.2 m) across, and the bob hung in the center. I leaned in and looked up. The bob hung down through a hole from the top of the warehouse.

"What's that," I asked. "Well, you see that circle?" my guide answered. "If you ever see the bob hanging outside that circle, run for the door. It's *creeling*." That's a word I've never heard anywhere else.

Heaven Hill master distiller Conor O'Driscoll confirmed it, though, just a month before I finished this manuscript. Creeling is when a warehouse leans past the recovery point and the weight of the barrels continues to pull it over. Time to head for the door and hope you picked the right one.

The Vaults is dim and chockablock with casks of varied sizes: here a bourbon barrel, there an extended port pipe, over there a hulking Madeira drum. The air is heavy with barrel breath, almost boozy. This is where some of the most prized barrels of Bowmore are kept, and to get a sampling here is a head-spinning experience.

Dunnage warehouses are a link to the past. Does that mean the whisky aged there has a more authentic flavor, is somehow more true and traditional? Not really. It's made the same way as the whisky racked in the modern warehouses. Is it better because of the dampness? Again you're looking at a choice the distillery manager makes.

Some barrels go in the dunnage warehouses, some go in the racked houses, and the blender takes them all. There are special warehouses like Bowmore's, and maybe the manager will sock away some promising barrels there, but it's more likely because the dunnage warehouses tend to be more steady state in their temperature and humidity and only change slowly. Or it's a large part of superstition, something a craft shaped by tradition can't completely ignore.

Japanese distillers also have a mix of old-style dunnage-type warehouses (low and cool but with concrete floors) and huge modern rack-style warehouses. Suntory recently built two warehouses capable of holding about 130,000 casks each, veritable supertankers of whisky warehouses.

The large Irish distillers have a similar mix. Bushmills is undergoing an expansion that may lead to more modern warehouses there. Midleton Distillery uses modern rackhouses almost exclusively and has them packed into a relatively small distillery campus. The new Tullamore Dew distillery is growing with new rack-style warehouses. Kilbeggan has one warehouse that's an odd one, a kind of big concrete Quonset hut–looking thing. Still the whiskey tastes fine, and the proof is in the drinking, so to speak.

Rackhouses and Rickhouses

The most common warehouse type for American whiskey at the larger end of the industry is what's known as an ironclad or a rackhouse.

An oak frame goes up with the racks built in as the structure is raised, three to nine stories high. Then the finished frame is covered in relatively thin sheets of corrugated metal. The 53-gallon (200.6 liters) American standard barrels are then rolled into the wooden racks on each floor, usually ten deep and three rows high.

You'll hear them called rackhouses or rickhouses. They're not *quite* the same thing. "Rickhouse" is a warehouse built using a patented system of Buzick Construction, the family-owned company that builds almost all of the ironclads in Kentucky. So while not every whiskey warehouse is a "rickhouse" (some of them predate the company's founding), there are so many that are that it's become a common name for it. But you'll hear "rackhouse" as well, and "warehouse," of course. The "almost" similarity of the words is as confusing as the use of either "setback" or "backset" for sour mash added to fermentation.

The Warehouse Zoo

Buffalo Trace Distillery sometimes resembles a living history exhibit more than a distillery. They're currently making whiskey in a copper-lined brick fermenter built in the 1870s that, until recently, was buried under a concrete floor in a building used for storage.

Their warehouses are a combination of old, new, and experimental. The old ones are a variety of brick, masonry, and concrete dating from the 1800s and the mid-1900s. Two of the latter were recently reclaimed from a past conversion to office space and are now holding barrels again. The different types of warehouses give master distiller Harlen Wheatley more flavor options when it comes to creating whiskeys.

But they have some novel, if not completely unique, warehouses as well. For example, Warehouse V is a tiny, one-barrel-capacity warehouse, that has traditionally housed the distillery's milestone barrels. The 7 millionth barrel was placed there with great fanfare in September 2018.

Warehouse P is a new idea in warehousing—a truly extreme project. Warehouse P is refrigerated and kept at a constant temperature of 45°F (7.2°C). The plan is to age bourbon (and other whiskeys;

Sazerac has distilleries and joint ventures all over the place) at this temperature for up to fifty years. This is a completely new idea, and no one really knows what to expect in terms of flavor creation.

They're also building regular ironclad warehouses—thirty of them, behemoths that will hold just under 69,000 barrels each—in an attempt to finally get ahead of the demand for their whiskeys. It's a major undertaking, but proper planning makes it possible.

Finally do you remember the "Tornado Surviving" bourbon they made at Buffalo Trace, from those barrels that were exposed to the elements after their warehouse was hit by a tornado in 2006? That got the folks at Buffalo Trace thinking: Do rackhouses really keep whiskey in optimum conditions?

So they built a small warehouse— Warehouse X, and be careful how you say that aloud—with five bays and a hugely expensive air-handling system. Experiments are done using barrels filled with their regular Buffalo Trace new make, a rye bourbon mashbill.

Each of four bays holds a maximum of thirty barrels and is subjected to different conditions: constant light, no light, constant temperature, high-volume airflow, no airflow, and so on. The fifth bay is essentially a breezeway with a roof and locked gates on either end, used as a control, similar to what the Tornado Surviving whiskey experienced.

Distillery president Mark Brown is excited about the idea of finding new ways to age whiskey. But at the same time he wryly notes the possibility of the control bay producing the best whiskey. "If we've been building warehouses all this time when we should have been just piling barrels in an open field with a tent overhead and a fence around them," he said, "we'll look like a bunch of proper monkeys." Monkeys in a warehouse zoo— brilliant, innovative proper monkeys.

These tall, broad warehouses can hold more than 50,000 barrels of aging whiskey, every one of them singing a slightly different song of aging, from the cool, mellow bass of the lower floors to the searing soprano soar of the top level. Much of that is driven by convection heating. As the summer sun beats down on that metal skin, the warehouse heats up; and "up" is the operative word. The heat, the hot air, will rise; and the top floor of a big warehouse can hit 135°F (57.2°C) in the summer. I know, I've been there. And although it's relatively dry, it will make the sweat pop right off your brow.

The heat expands the whiskey, drives it hard and deep into the red layer, picking up more than just the regular load of sugars and vanillins, getting into more tannins. In the industry, these barrels, these top floors produce whiskey that is known as "high and dry," referring to the bracing, lean character. This is where you get the leather, heat, and fiery oak spice. It's happening faster, too; and the barrels are giving up a much higher percentage to evaporation. You can almost get buzzed taking a deep breath.

Evan Williams 23 Year Old

Export bottling of a classically "high & dry" bourbon. Sharply oaked nose, hot, and a bit sweet. Flashing hot on the tongue, oak and dry corn, some acidity. Long dry finish. Water smooths and sweetens it significantly.

Cycling Warehouses

Brown-Forman has a number of masonry and brick warehouses at their Shively and Versailles (Woodford Reserve) sites that they call "cycling" warehouses.

In a process that dates back to the 1800s, they use steam heat during the cold weather to slowly bring the warehouses up to about 80°F (26.7°C) over a period of roughly ten days, and then allow it to sink back to the mid-50s Fahrenheit (low teens Celsius) over the next ten days, and then start the cycle again. Buffalo Trace Distillery has been steam-heating their brick warehouses in a similar fashion since 1886.

This is something that's not done with the typical ironclad warehouse, and for good reason. The uninsulated metal walls would make it an exercise in heating the outdoors. The old-style, solid-wall warehouses hold the heat and allow for an economy of energy use.

Interesting, but do they affect the flavor? The assumption most drinkers jump to is that cycling warehouses are an attempt to speed up aging by continuing the in-out extraction of flavor from the wood that happens during the warmer months, even in the depths of winter. Such as those depths are in Kentucky, that is.

Brown-Forman master distiller Chris Morris and I were in one of the cycling warehouses a while back, and I asked him about that. He said that it's not about aging the whiskey faster, or better, but differently. "It does make a difference," I remember him saying.

Brown-Forman and Morris have these warehouses and their own cooperage right there in Louisville. The Brown family has always felt free to take chances with innovation through the years, Morris and his team have both the opportunity and the will to play around with wood-aging tricks, and they take that chance often with things like various wine finishes on Woodford and the new Coopers' Craft bourbon aged in grooved barrels.

Heating warehouses full of barrels of whiskey by as much as 30°F (16.7°C) takes a lot of steam and that's not cheap. If they weren't getting an impact on flavor from it, I doubt they'd be doing it.

🥃 *Woodford Reserve*

A mix of pot and column still whiskey, all aged in cycling warehouses. Woodford is rich with vanilla, roasted nuts, baking spice, and toffee, with brighter notes and firm oak on the palate.

The lower floors stay cooler, both because of the heat rising and because of the intake of fresh air to replace the rising hot air that's fueling the top-floor inferno. Some blenders will skip over these barrels; some use these floors (or rent them) for aging spirits other than whiskey. If you're drinking a bourbon or rye that's more than twenty years old, chances are good that it spent those years down here, cruising along on a slower course to maturity.

Are they forgotten? No, but while they will develop deeper wood notes, without the dry brightness of the hotter barrels, the chances of over-aging into heavy acetone notes are less. These barrels are not particularly sweet either because of the lower extraction.

Meanwhile, in the middle floors, as you'd expect, the barrels are hitting a balance. Oak tones are strong but not burly or piercing. Sweetness is bigger here, where the extraction is active without digging deep enough to mine additional tannins. This is where a lot of the distillers will find their favorite "honey barrels."

Top to bottom in the warehouse, you'll find plenty of difference in the same distillate in the same type of barrels. This makes the biggest difference, but there are more. Barrels will age differently by how close they are to the southern-facing wall, which gets more sun. The prevailing winds will make a difference in an ironclad. There are brick

warehouses with closed floors, where the airflow is all horizontal and the differences between the floors are less. Everything makes a difference in how long a barrel is hot, how swiftly it cools, and how much airflow it gets, all of which impact evaporative loss and wood extraction.

Airing out a warehouse

Cave of Wonder

I hate the phrase "the most unique." Unique means "singular." Either there's one of something and it's unique, or there's more than one and it's not.

But I'm going to use it because the aging cave at Maker's Mark is the most unique whiskey warehouse I've ever seen. The concrete half-pipe at Kilbeggan is weird, and the steel-railed whiskey box at the new Old Forester distillery in downtown Louisville is downright cinematic. But both must give way to The Cellar.

Maker's Mark produces their Maker's 46, a collaboration with Independent Stave Company that transforms their bourbon by aging it for six weeks post-maturity with the addition of ten toasted oak staves hung in the whisky on a food-grade plastic-and-steel insert in the barrel. It's great stuff, but they soon realized that the barrels they'd "extra-aged" over the winter tasted a lot better. The warmer months led to over extraction. As distillery president emeritus Bill Samuels Jr. put it, it didn't "taste yummy" anymore.

The decision was made to continue production of the Maker's 46 and to keep it cool, so the decision was made to dynamite a big hole in the hill on the distillery grounds. It was fitted with impressively huge doors, racks, and glass interior walls. Maker's Mark runs their Private Select tasting sessions in the cave, where groups buying a barrel can pick their own special blend of staves to hang in a barrel of Maker's. (I've done it, with three other whiskey writers. We called it the Curmudgeon's Blend, and it was delicious—and a lot of fun to do.)

The Whisky Cave of Wonder: amazing what a warehouse can do and be.

 Maker's 46

Maker's 46 adds toasted staves as a finish. Rich sweet corn and leather with oak heat on the nose. Flavors of vanilla, caramel, toasted corn with an oak frame, sliding into a sweet, warm finish.

Entrance to tthe Maker's Mark cellar (Loretto, KY)

There's a variety in how the rickhouses are sited that I find intriguing. Warehouses may be high on a hill to catch the prevailing wind or lower down to avoid tornadoes. They may be aligned north-south to maximize the amount of sunlight on the broad sidewalls or aligned east-west so the prevailing winds blow through the doors. Some have windows; some do not. A warehouse may be built by a stream or river to get the cool air or well away from a river to avoid the damp.

Buffalo Trace Distillery's Warehouse X

All of these decisions are the result of a distiller's experience with previous warehouses and whiskey. I think of it as "Kentucky feng shui," similar to the Chinese ideas of how to orient a building auspiciously. Some make sense, like the one about keeping the trees and bushes clear around the warehouses. It keeps the light regular, and no tree is going to get high enough to fall on the warehouse.

Most of them, though, come down to something the late Parker Beam, longtime Heaven Hill master distiller, told me about the idea. "That's just one guy saying, 'This worked for me, that's why I do it,' and another guy saying, 'Oh hell, that don't work at all.'" Sounds familiar, doesn't it? Siting your warehouse is another choice about whiskey flavor.

I saved my favorite influence on American whiskey warehouses for last. The late Ronnie Eddins, the longtime warehouse manager at Buffalo Trace Distillery, told me that he was sure the regular fog off the Kentucky River beside the warehouses—and the way it would wetly come right in the windows—gave his whiskey a "sweeter, more mellow taste." Well, why not? It's not like we can explain everything about whiskey.

Warehouses can provide a wide range of character to bourbon and rye. We'll talk more about this in the blending chapter. This is how different bourbons are made from the same mashbill, fermentation, distillation, and barrel choice. They say that 70 percent of bourbon and rye flavor comes from the barrel, but it's really the combination of the barrel and the time it spends in the warehouse.

Low Houses

While other bourbon distillers are building five- and seven-story rackhouses and blending great, yet different, bourbons from the variety created by those temperature and airflow differences, Four Roses ages every bit of their whiskey in single-story, steel-walled warehouses, sometimes known as "flat houses." They're relatively small and are clustered fairly tightly in a few areas down in Bourbon Country.

What's the story? Four Roses, like Maker's Mark, is trying to keep the aging process from affecting barrels differently. Maker's does this because they only have one brand that's coming straight from the barrel. The other Maker's Mark bottlings, like 46 and the Private Select line, vary by the use of an additional process.

But Four Roses relies on their unique system of blending ten different straight bourbon barrelings that derive from their two mashbills and five yeast strains. They want the whiskey from each of these ten varieties to be as uniform as possible, so they limit the differences created by larger warehouses by keeping their whiskey in single-floor, smaller warehouses. This keeps the heat and air circulation the same for each barrel, as much as is possible. It's another flavor choice.

Bonded

Canadian distillers refer to groups of barrels as "bonds." This stems from the days when everything had to go into a bonded warehouse, locked by a government agent. They still call the lots of barrels chosen for blending as bonds, I guess because they all move together.

Canadian warehouses tend to be low and wide, single-story affairs; but there are brick warehouses in urban settings and some multifloor warehouses. They are no longer bonded, but they are often palletized. This makes it easier, much easier, to move barrels in and out of the warehouse. Strapped to pallets four at a time, the barrels can be stacked to the ceiling, essentially supporting themselves.

There are some downsides to palletizing. Air circulation tends to be lower in palletized warehouses, as the stacks of barrels are placed in proximity to help support each other. An upside to vertical aging is that, as the whisky evaporates, it continues to touch every stave, so it may minimize losses. That said, Crown Royal did years of comparison taste tests before converting from horizontal racks to palletization, and they said they found no difference. I've been impressed with their tasting prowess, so I'll tip my hat to that.

I will say that Canadian distillers don't seem to open their warehouses as often as some of the other distillers do. I've only been in seven or eight Canadian warehouses (the distilleries don't offer tours, as a rule), but each one has been a matter of opening the door and being hit by a tidal wave of boozy air.

It's actually not funny. One I was in led me to quickly check my shoes to be sure I didn't have any protruding metal; I was afraid of creating a spark. I was accompanied into a Crown Royal warehouse by a technician holding a sensing device. We got about a third of the way into the building when she suddenly said, "No, that's it, we have to leave." The box was flashing red; the alcohol level was too high.

What's going on there? Holding in alcohol also means they're holding in the heat, leading to greater extraction. But it's Canada, and even in the summer, on the prairie, it's not hot like Kentucky. So you've got greater extraction, but it's pulling out more sugars and caramel. You're not getting the "high and dry" effect you get in Kentucky.

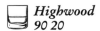

Highwood
90 20

This spends twenty years in a boozy Canadian warehouse. Rich nose of butterscotch and hot caramel with cedar spikes. Lots of vanilla and caramel, light butterscotch, and just a hint of the cedar into the finish.

Mother of Invention

Craft distillers are often working on a shoestring, and it shows. The distillery may be in a sketchy part of town or way out in the country because the rents are lower there. There may be a great address but a tasting bar made of repurposed pallets to save money. The fermenters are often food-grade plastic totes, the ubiquitous intermediate-sized shipping containers used for syrups, grains, and other free-flowing cargo.

The "warehouse" is often just a room, or a corner of a larger room, stacked with barrels on steel racks. As mentioned at the start of the chapter, some distillers use shipping containers, some use pole barns, and some use truck trailers. The aim is to get all your barrels somewhere that's lockable, safe from sparks, and subject to temperature swings.

As inventory grows, or if these distillers transition fully to 53-gallon (200.6 liters) American standard barrels, expansion is necessary. Some distillers lease space; some build it. The hard part is keeping things consistent: If you were aging in a shipping container in the sun, you don't want to suddenly go to a concrete building in a shaded valley. It will change the flavor of your whiskey.

One of the more interesting quirks to warehousing was an old technique revived by the Jefferson's brand. They put some of their barrels on a ship, so they went through the rocking and temperature changes that happened on the voyage. Different ships and different routes seemed to make for different bourbons. Fremont Mischief Distillery in Seattle took a slightly different tack: They put barrels of their rye out on Alaskan fishing boats to create different variants of what they called Storm Tossed rye.

Warehouses can be on hills, by rivers, by the ocean. They may be in wooded glades, wide-open fields, or city streets.

They can be made of wood, brick, or stone; short or toweringly tall. It can all affect the whiskey inside. In the next chapter, we'll put the whiskey in the barrel, and then in the warehouse, and see what happens when you add the critical ingredient: time.

Fremont Capt. Sig Hansen's Storm Tossed Rye

Aged two seasons on board Hansen's F/V *Northwestern* in the Bering Sea. Bright floral notes, cough lozenges on the nose. Medicinal and sweet with a crisp mineral flash to it. Unique.

Low, small-barrel warehouse at Ranger Creek Brewing & Distilling (San Antonio, TX)

The Time

We've made the whiskey, which took less than a week from milling to mashing to the completion of fermentation. We distilled it, which took maybe two days at most. We put it in barrels, which even at a small distillery doesn't take more than a couple minutes per barrel, including hammering in the bung. Then we loaded it on a truck (or rolled it by hand or used a forklift), took it to the warehouse, and put it in place, deciding the right place for this particular barrel, and recording where it was put. Ten days, tops.

And then we wait. It might be for months at a startup craft distillery, it might be for forty years or more at a Scotch or Canadian distillery. However long it is, in almost every warehouse, the only thing that's going to disturb that barrel's slumber is the occasional sampling.

It certainly looks like nothing's happening on a day-to-day basis. The barrel sits there, a big lump of steel-bound wood in a long line of big lumps of steel-bound wood, not moving.

There are obvious clues that something is going on. The biggest one is the smell: the rich, ripe roll of aroma that says "whiskey warehouse." If nothing was going on, there would be no smell at all. The smell proves that the oak is "breathing." The slightly permeable wood is doing its job, allowing a slow exchange of air from the outside with water and alcohol (and wood aromatics) from the inside. That's an essential part of whiskey maturation, another amazing thing that happens naturally—like the reaction of copper with sulfur-bearing compounds in distillation—to make whiskey better, to make whiskey even possible.

Another clue is the presence on some barrels of slow, sticky leaks from between the staves. I call that "barrel drool" or "barrel candy." The whiskey will leak at a slow enough pace that very little additional loss is taking place, compared to the "angel's share" losses of evaporation exchange; but it does make for a sweet, sweet smell in the warehouse.

I remember being in the warehouse at A. Smith Bowman Distillery one time with the late Truman Cox, who'd recently become master distiller there. We came across a barrel that was leaking pretty heavily, and he licked his finger, ran it slowly along one of the leaks, and licked it again. "Go on," he urged me, "it's good!" I did, and you know, it was sticky and a little dusty, but it was good: caramel, maple syrup, vanilla, a bit of burnt sugar.

We know the barrels are doing something because we can smell and see bits of evidence on the outside. What's really going on inside while the whiskey slumbers? The actual magnitude of the number of chemical interactions going on inside a barrel of whiskey is dizzying and far beyond the scope of a work such as this. Research continues, and the fullness of what happens as a whiskey ages may never fully be known.

The thing to avoid is focusing on one set of reactions over another, the type of tunnel vision we're specifically trying to move beyond. In this case, when the number of possibilities is almost literally endless, the best we can do is acknowledge that and touch on the major classes of actions that are going on.

First Things First

The first and fastest thing that happens is color extraction. Unless a barrel is a second or third refill, the new make whiskey is going to pull a lot of color out of the wood in the first few months.

The extraction rate is even faster in the smaller barrels favored by some craft distillers due to the higher ratio of wood surface to volume of spirit.

The color comes partly from the color already in the wood. You can see that in lakes that are fed by streams or bogs that have tannin-bearing vegetation in them, often fallen trees: willows, pines, and oak. The lake waters will be dark with the tannins, almost like strong tea.

The color is also coming from the heat-treated part of the barrel: the red layer. The caramelized sugars are leaching out of the wood into the spirit, and the color comes with them. This is the same kind of caramel used to add color to whiskies, but those sugars come from malt, not wood.

 Ranger Creek .36 Texas Bourbon

Aging in 5- and 10-gallon (18.9 and 37.9 liters) barrels in Texas heat speeds up the color conversion. Very dark color and an oaky-sweet nose. Oak and corn sweetness dialed up to 12, but the head-to-head battle is a prize fight, engrossing and brutally delicious.

As explained in the previous chapter on the barrel, flavor and aroma are also coming directly out of the wood. Simple chemical extraction from the solvent effect of the alcohol and water is pulling flavor out of the wood itself and also the red layer.

Used barrels are giving up the flavor that's left in the wood, and any flavor from the liquid they may have held previously—whiskey, wine, rum, whatever—is mixing in as well. That would seem to be

added flavor, and the different national whiskey regulations address that in different ways.

Besides simple extraction, flavor is being created in the barrel over time by chemical interactions among the alcohol, the various polymers in the wood (hemicellulose and lignin chief among them), acids and esters in the wood and the distillate, higher alcohols (called "fusel oils"), and more than 200 different compounds that are reacting in this oaken crucible. Aging whiskey in containers other than wood simply wouldn't result in whiskey, not because of regulations but because of the amazing array of flavors that are in the oak or created in the oak by air-drying, toasting, and charring, and the flavors created by the interaction among components of the wood and the distillate.

Flavor is also created by the slow interaction with the outside environment. That's the evaporation of alcohol and water that slowly moves out of the barrel, almost like an extreme slow-motion distillation, that we romantically call the "angel's share."

The Angel's Share

You've all heard the term; I've used it already in earlier chapters. It's a romantic imagining of where the evaporating whiskey goes when it escapes the barrel.

If you've ever been in a whiskey warehouse, it's pretty obvious where the whiskey goes; it's all around you, sometimes so heavy in the air you can catch a buzz just walking around. That's no exaggeration; I toured one warehouse with two other writers, and afterward we decided we'd best walk to lunch rather than drive.

The longer whiskey is in a barrel, the more it will evaporate. A reused barrel will lose whiskey faster; a smaller barrel will lose it faster. The loss will be slower in cool or wet climates; it will be frighteningly fast in tropical climates—but it never stops. It is the true end point of aging a whiskey. Eventually the angels "share" so much that either the whiskey goes below legal proof limits (more likely in cold climates) or it simply disappears in an oaky cloud as astringent vapor.

Horrible as that is, it is necessary for whiskey maturation. Without this exchange, the whiskey simply will not mature properly. The oxygen and heat that come into the barrel

drive chemical change (which is why accelerated aging schemes often center on these two factors). Oxygenation reduces astringency, creates new flavors from tannins, and also increases color.

This oxygenation through the wooden walls of the barrel is a big reason why distillers can't "age" whiskey by pumping it into a huge stainless-steel tank with a bunch of charred wood chips or spirals. A tank is much cheaper than using wooden barrels, but it's not permeable. And an oak barrel, as I said elsewhere, is just waterproof enough.

There are so many flavors and aromas that come from aging whiskey in oak barrels, and the paths that create those flavors and aromas are so complex that they have not all been recorded. Like so many other things to do with whiskey, there comes a point in aging where science still has to step aside and give way to art and empirical knowledge. "If we do it this way, it smells like this" is still the way to make whiskey.

Refills Are Slow

It's well known that American whiskeys are, for the most part, aged in new, charred oak barrels. Bourbon and rye whiskey must be, by regulation.

Most other whiskeys are aged in used barrels, and most of those are ex-bourbon barrels. The first filling usually pulls a generous amount of flavor— vanilla, coconut, caramel—and some color from the wood.

Clearly, the second filling has less to work with after the barrel has already had spirit in it. The color is quite a bit slower to accumulate, and if the whiskey is left uncolored, with no added caramel, even a 20 year old aged in a second-fill cask can be quite pale. The flavor is also harder to come by, and the whiskey will have less of the identifying tastes of the cask—being more about the flavors of oxygenation— and may well taste a lot more like the new make spirit, with a lot of distillery character.

We talked about the oxidation in the chapter on barrels, but there's more to it; it works better in the right used, tired barrels. I learned this from Matt Hoffmann, the distiller at Westland Distillery in Seattle: Air-dried wood works better in refill barrels than kiln-dried wood.

"It's one of the most important things but one that no one really knows about," he told me. "After a point, the oxidation doesn't take place unless you have a catalyst. Oxygen occurs naturally as O_2, but oxidation takes place with only a single oxygen atom. Without a catalyst [to split the molecule], you won't get the effect.

"That's one of the benefits of air drying," he continued. "It creates phenolic acids that drive that oxidation. When you have every other variable equal, you'll have more development in whiskey in air-dried wood, whereas kiln-dried wood doesn't drive that."

It's complicated. You don't know what's going to affect what, and it all drives the flavor.

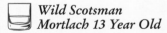 *Wild Scotsman Mortlach 13 Year Old*

Single malt aged in ex-bourbon casks and quite pale. Honey and hard candies with a touch of heat on the nose. Vanilla and dark caramel, spicy oak notes, pepper and dark cookies on the palate with a long sweet/spice finish.

Size Matters

*The size of a barrel will affect the aging rate.
It also has an effect on the economics, so you have
to be somewhat careful when making judgments
about barrel sizes.*

The larger the barrel, the longer the aging process takes, and the lower the evaporation rate.

That's a trade-off, with longer time costing more and lower evaporation saving money. Counterintuitively, larger barrels actually take up less room in a warehouse, because the volume is a square of the radius of the barrel. Larger barrels cost less per unit of volume, so there are substantial savings to be had by using larger barrels.

It's not only about economics, though. Past a point, larger barrels don't lose enough whiskey through evaporation for the maturation process to work at an optimal rate, and the surface-to-volume ratio is too low for effective wood extraction. They also become prohibitively heavy and harder to move and concentrate valuable whiskey into a container that's more likely to tip and shatter when being moved. The largest casks regularly used in aging whiskey are port pipes (550 liters [145.3 gallons]) and Madeira drums (up to 650 liters [171.7 gallons]), but

most whiskey is aged in casks of 200 to 250 liters 52.8 to 66 gallons) in size.

At the other end of the scale are the small barrels craft distillers use, which may be as small as 2 gallons (7.6 liters). There are quite a few 10- and 15-gallon (37.9 and 56.8 liters) barrels in use by small distillers. The idea is to age the whiskey more quickly. With the much higher surface-to-volume ratio, the spirit gains color and flavor rapidly; but the question is whether the flavors are all desirable. Tasters talk about "small-barrel character," an excessively tannic note that can overwhelm the spirit flavor.

The smaller barrels also have cost issues. The price is almost as high as full-sized barrels—the labor is the same or greater—and the evaporative loss is quite a bit faster. I've heard of 10-gallon (37.9 liters) barrels being almost empty at five years old. That's not all bad, as small-barrel whiskeys are mostly American and spending that time in new, charred oak; so two years' aging is usually about as much as you want to subject them to. More than that and the barrel can get overwhelming.

There's a more subtle issue with the flavor and character of the small barrels. I've got a buddy who's a whiskey chemist, Scott Spolverino, who describes the difference as aged versus matured. "Aging is what you put on the bottle: How old is it?" he said. "It has more to do with wood compounds, wood-based flavors, more extraction, and literally the time it's in there. Maturation is the culmination of chemical reactions and evaporation."

There's also a physical process that takes time, and the size of the barrel has nothing to do with it. It's called "ethanol clustering," a structural integration of ethanol and water that makes the ethanol sensation on the palate smoother. "A small barrel can't force the hand here," he said. No matter what your whiskey snob friends tell you, apparently, "smooth" really is a word to describe a mature whiskey!

All that said, I've had some small-barrel American whiskeys that are quite good. Distillers have learned to use what the small barrels have to offer and adjust their spirit accordingly. Some distillers use the small barrels only when they're getting started, to have something to bottle and sell quickly and get some cash in the door, then transition to larger 30-gallon (113.6 liters) or standard 53-gallon (200.6 liters) barrels. But some stick with at least some small barrels to add to the blend, maintaining the flavor that their fans first gravitated toward.

 Kings County Peated Bourbon

Kings County has stuck with small barrels. Peat, green corn, and shiny oak. Hot, peaty, fresh corn finish slides into sweetness and gentle smoke.

Tempus Fugit

Barrels aren't cheap, warehouses are big money, and taxes never go down. But the biggest expense in making whiskey is time.

It takes time to make good whiskey, most definitely; but while that time passes— months, years, decades—the whiskey makes you no money at all. It *costs* you money: warehouse maintenance, security, warehouse staff, and taxes, taxes, and more taxes. What's worse, it's not just sitting there losing you money. It's literally evaporating, disappearing at a rate of 1 to 10 percent a year! Sure that's necessary to the development of mature whiskey, but it's also necessary to have mature whiskey to sell.

Is it any wonder that distillers have constantly been tempted to cheat time by speeding up the aging process for whiskey?

Distillers in the past tried heating the barrels (not cycling, *heating*), bubbling oxygen through the whiskey, ultrasonic agitation—and those are only the schemes I've heard of. None of them worked. How do I know that? Because everyone is still putting whiskey in barrels and stacking them in warehouses.

Almost everyone. There's a new wave of accelerated-aging experimentation going on. Distillers are trying sonic agitation: vibrating the whiskey to accelerate the progress of aging. There are elaborate plans for removing certain chemicals, adjusting levels of others, smashing the whiskey with high-intensity lights, and so on. And yes, they're still bubbling oxygen through the whiskey.

Does it work? That depends on what you want the processes to do. If you expect to get the equivalent of a $100 bottle of 15-year-old bourbon in six months, or a 20-year-old Islay in under a year, well, currently, that's not going to happen. (It's interesting that all the accelerated aging schemes I know of are about making bourbon or malt whiskey, usually peated malt whiskey.) I've tasted a variety of accelerated-age whiskeys—some blind, some open label—and I've been unimpressed. I picked out the quickie whiskeys four times out of five in the blind tasting.

If, on the other hand, you're fed up with paying $50 for a good blended Scotch, or you want a bottle of bourbon for making highballs over the weekend and don't want to pay a lot for it, then there might be a market for this stuff. Some distillers are aiming higher than that, and they've got a ways to go, in my opinion. But some distillers are looking to make commodity whiskey, and that's within reach.

One guy stuck to a pretty simple method. Rick Wasmund, at Copper Fox Distillery in Sperryville, in the mountains of Virginia, wanted to get more wood character into his 100 percent malt whiskey. When he puts it in the barrel, he adds a mesh sack of wood chips: oak and fruitwood, like apple or peach. The sack stays in twelve months, and the whiskey's in the barrel for an additional two months or so. It comes out surprisingly smooth and tasty for a malt whiskey under two years old.

As is true with any bottle you buy, you need to know what's in it. Who made it, and what are you paying for? Like I keep saying, it's all about making choices.

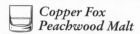

Copper Fox Peachwood Malt

Finished with a "tea bag" of peachwood chips. Nose is sweet, doughy, and shot with green wood. Dry malt on the tongue, hints of the peachwood coming through, and a fruity finish, tapering off to oak dryness.

TEMPUS FUGIT

How Old?

We're taught that asking someone's age directly is rude. Whiskey sometimes makes it easy by putting the age right on the label. It's a little bit complicated in that if there is an age on the label, say, fifteen years old, that means that the youngest whiskey that's in the mix that went into that bottling is fifteen years old.

There may be older whiskeys in there as well (though to be honest, in current times, that's nowhere near as likely as it was twenty years ago, when there was a bit of a glut of aged whiskeys) because the blender can bring a touch of complex depth to a bottling by adding some more mature whiskey to it.

What if there isn't an age statement? There are quite a few no age statement (NAS) whiskeys these days, and it seems to me that there are more than there used to be. That's more than likely due to the shortage of whiskey stocks, a direct result of people like you and me talking more people into trying good whiskey—because then they go out and buy more whiskey, which means less for us!

The smug and cynical believe that there are more NAS bottlings because we're being sold younger whiskey as a way for the distillers to save money. I've seen drinkers opine that age statements are important as gauges of whiskey value, how much a whiskey is truly worth.

Distillers counter that NAS whiskeys are not blended by the clock; they're blended when the flavors are ready. They also point out that there are some NAS bottlings that draw plenty of critical acclaim and mad love from their drinkers: Ardbeg Uigeadail, Lot No. 40, Booker's, Jameson Rarest Vintage Reserve, and the new Nikka from the Barrel.

In the next chapter, on blending, we'll take a look at how blenders choose the whiskeys that go into a bottling, including how a 15-year-old single malt isn't necessarily the same 12-year-old single malt, only three years older. For our purposes here, if it says fifteen years old, it's at least that old, period.

What about those 30-year-old, 40-year-old, and even 50-year-old Scotch whiskies? I had a 41-year-old Canadian not long ago that was pretty darned special, too. Why aren't bourbons aged that long? What about Irish whiskeys? Are they just not as good? Bite your tongue. Of course they're good. The Irish distillers have bottled some old whiskeys, and they're awesome; but they're usually working more on spirit balance than barrel.

 Lot No. 40

Lot No. 40 is done when it's done: No age statement. Rye and oak march arm in arm out of the glass, with some dried pit fruits in the background. Rich oak and leather layer with the rye snap and caramel sweetness. Who cares how old it is?

Do fewer labels with age statements mean we're drinking younger whiskies? Not necessarily.

Climate Change

While we're talking about how much faster bourbon ages in Kentucky's hot climate, step back a moment and consider what it's like for Kavalan (Taiwan), Amrut Distillery (India), Paul John (India), and Rampur Distillery (India) when they have to age their whiskies in climates hundreds of miles closer to the equator. It's hot at the distilleries and even hotter in their warehouses. Paul John, in Goa, India, built an underground warehouse to even things out a bit.

These distillers are faced with greedy angels, losing more than 10 percent a year to evaporation in the brutal heat. But balance that with whisky that matures—magnificently, in some cases—in a matter of three to five years, and you can see the appeal of that trade-off. These relatively young companies have mastered their natural aging acceleration situation quite handily (Kavalan had the help of the late Dr. Jim Swan, an acknowledged master of wood science). I know I'm happy to sample any of their whiskies when I see them.

A distiller like Mackmyra has different problem. Mackmyra is in Sweden, about 110 miles (177 km) north of Stockholm, so their whisky ages more slowly. They've taken to using more interesting wood in their barrels to get more flavor into the whisky. Other Scandinavian distillers, faced with the same issues, have been using small barrels.

American whiskeys have a whole different *gestalt*. I've said this so many times about different whiskeys. Whiskey drinkers who stick to one type either want to measure all other whiskeys by those standards or simply not try them at all. It shouldn't work that way.

Consider bourbon's world. American whiskey ferments and distills on the grain, making for a more beefy distillate. They are aged in new charred-oak barrels, which put a lot of huge flavor into the whiskey. Then consider the American climate, particularly in Kentucky, when compared to Scotland, Canada, Ireland, or Japan. It's not only a new barrel; the whiskey's getting slammed into it by raging hot summers, concentrated at the top of a seven-story ironclad warehouse.

If you tried to keep that up for forty years, you'd wind up with a barrel with maybe a pint of whiskey left, dark as tar, and tasting like burnt wood. It simply doesn't work. As for me, I'd just as soon have a 6- or 8-year-old bourbon—or a 2-year-old rye!—because that's more in the sweet spot for that spirit and for my tastes.

The more you know about how a whiskey is made and how it fits into its own category, the more you'll understand how it tastes and how good a job the distiller and blender did in creating it.

Finishing

Back in the late 1980s and early 1990s, in a surprising display of synchronicity, a few Scottish master blenders came up with the same idea at about the same time. After aging a single malt to maturity in one type of cask—an ex-bourbon barrel, for example—they would transfer the whisky to a different type of cask, maybe an ex-sherry or ex-port. The whisky developed the flavors and aromas of the bourbon barrel, then had a layer of fruit and nuts laid on top of it.

It was a success, and more "finishing"—as it came to be called generally—spread throughout the industry, eventually crossing over to the other whiskey-making regions. There were a few issues with labeling, as some regulators saw the introduction of a new type of aging vessel as a deliberate attempt to add flavor, when that was against some countries' regulations; but everyone found a way to make it happen.

Some worked better than others. I recall a Tokaji-finished peat monster of an Islay single malt that was, well, ill-advised. Of course, I loved the Woodford Reserve that was finished in Sonoma-Cutrer chardonnay barrels; not many people agreed with me on that one. There was a St. George malt that was finished in pear eau-de-vie casks that was stunning.

Finished whiskeys have become part of the landscape, another way of adding interesting flavor to the glass. The wild exuberance of the blenders for different finishes has subsided a bit, but experiments continue, and the future undoubtedly holds more surprises.

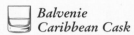

Balvenie Caribbean Cask

A 14-year-old single malt finished in rum casks. Vanilla, Demerara sugar, and lush fruit leap out of the glass. It's clearly whisky on the tongue—malt, fruit, oak—but the framing is all rum: brown sugar, vanilla, and higher fruity notes. Nice balance.

The Blend

It's time to talk about one of the final steps: blending. I can see some of you making a face. You don't like blended whiskey? You think it's some kind of lesser whiskey, good only for mixing with soda and ice?

My friends, if you feel that way, you're missing out on beauties like Jameson Rarest Vintage Reserve, Canadian Club Chronicles, Royal Salute 21, Hibiki 21. You're also missing out on excellent single malts, single pot still whiskeys, and great bourbons. Worst of all, you're missing out on the simple pleasure of a tall highball, a cold and clanking glass of ice, mixer, and totally refreshing whiskey!

Part of understanding "blending" is understanding "blended." Let's take that on first.

One of the saddest things I hear otherwise sophisticated and well-informed whiskey drinkers say, particularly in America, is that a blended whiskey someone else might be talking about is just "brown vodka." The implication is that the whiskey is cheaply made by adding a small amount of whiskey to a large amount of neutral spirits that were run off a column still at vodka strength.

The nub of the issue is that in American whiskey terminology, American whiskey regulations, that's what a blended whiskey is. This is from our old friend, the Code of Federal Regulations, Title 27, Subpart C, Section 5.22, the "standards of identity."

"Blended whisky" (whisky—a blend) is a mixture that contains straight whisky or a blend of straight whiskies at not less than 20 percent on a proof gallon basis, excluding alcohol derived from added harmless coloring, flavoring or blending materials, and, separately, or in combination, whisky or neutral spirits.

A bottle being filled from a bourbon barrel using a whiskey thief.

In other words, to be labeled "blended whiskey" in America, all you have to do is put one part whiskey in your blend, along with four parts "neutral spirits." Neutral spirits are what's referred to in the trade as GNS (or NGS), which is "grain neutral spirits" (or "neutral grain spirits," same thing). A distiller can buy bulk GNS from a specialist manufacturer for an equivalent cost of less than a dollar per 750 ml bottle. If that's 80 percent of your "blended whiskey," then the price goes way down, along with flavor and complexity.

That's why blended whiskey brands aren't so big in the United States anymore. The only American blended whiskey of any size is Seagram's 7 Crown, which still puts up a respectable 2 million cases a year. (It was selling eight million cases in the 1970s.)

Assuming that "blended whiskey" means the same thing everywhere is an easy error. But you're smarter than that. America is the only one of the major whiskey regions where blends can be such debased mixtures.

 ### Seagram's 7

25 percent whiskey, 75 percent GNS. Aromas are mostly alcohol sweet, with some vanilla and brown sugar. Light mouthfeel and, again, sweet with some heat. Best as a mixer.

7&7 and Boilo

I took a slap at American blended whiskey in this chapter. I did. I called it a "debased mixture."

I spoke too soon. There are uses for American blends—fun and tasty ones. The best known is the iconic 7&7, a highball mix of Seagram's 7 Crown and 7-Up, with a lemon slice if you want. I remember drinking a lot of those in college. We were young sophisticates, drinking cocktails! The drink is pale gold in color, fizzy, and sweet with citrus notes from the soda, and just enough whiskey in there to let you know you're drinking, while the GNS provides the power.

But there's also Boilo, a traditional holiday punch from the coal regions of northeast Pennsylvania. I have a family recipe I got from a friend. Boilo is served hot to guests arriving in the winter's chill. The punch base is water, sugar and honey, caraway, cloves, cinnamon sticks, cut whole oranges, and 0.5 gallon (1.75 liters) of "cheap whiskey, the cheaper the better." The traditional add is Four Queens 101, a blended whiskey made by Laird (the Applejack people).

I've made Boilo, too; and like the 7&7, it's a fun drink—juicy and pleasant. And here's the thing that makes these drinks special and worth your attention: They are very social drinks. Hand someone a coffee mug full of steaming Boilo at a holiday get-together or a dewy-cold tumbler of 7&7 at a rocking house party, and I guarantee that no one's going to be stopping the party to ask you what whiskey you put in it. They'll sip, smile, and keep on talking. Whiskey's really good at that, too: blended, straight, or any other way you choose it.

This Is Blending

With that out of the way, let's talk about what
"blended whiskey" means for the rest of the world.

Without getting bogged down in details, the major difference is that the blends are made from actual whiskey, as we defined it back in chapter 1: a drink made from fermented grain that is then distilled, and aged in wooden barrels.

Pay close attention to those last four words. That's the big difference, you see. It all goes back to the regulations. American regulations only require that "whisky" spend an unspecified amount of time in oak to be considered whiskey. Pabst recently released a whiskey with an age statement of five seconds, a beautiful tongue-in-cheek example. But in Scotland, Ireland, and Canada, whiskey has to age for a minimum of three years for it to be allowed to be labeled as "whiskey" (Japan also currently has no age requirement for whiskey.)

Irish blended whiskey, like Jameson, for instance, is a mix of malt whiskey, single pot still whiskey, or both with grain whiskey. Grain whiskey, you'll recall, is mashed from a variety of cereals, fermented, and distilled in a continuous still to a very high proof, usually just under 96

percent ABV. (I've nosed Canadian new make at that point, and it is, amazingly, still possible to distinguish the base grain at that proof.) The grain whiskey is barreled, then aged for at least three years. Almost every drop is used for blended whiskeys.

It's the same with blended Scotch whisky, and almost every Canadian whisky. There's a whisky that's made in a pot still, distilled to a relatively low proof. Then there's a whisky that's made on a column still to a high proof. Both are aged in barrels for at least three years and then used for making blended whisky.

Why is it done this way? I could be cynical and say, "Because millions of people like drinking it that way"; but that's being a bit backward. People like it because each whisky in the blend brings something, and the whole is greater than the sum of the parts. In that way, blending does actually create flavors and doesn't merely put them together.

Let's start with that simplest of additions to the blending. Grain whisky is often said to add "mouthfeel" or "creaminess."

Grain whisky is light in flavor—I can attest to that—but aging in used oak does lend it some body, some flavors and attributes that add to fullness in the mouth.

If it were that simple, blenders would simply dump in the needed percentage of grain whisky from one distillery, one lot, and that would be that. But instead, there are often three or more grain whiskies added.

In Canada, for instance, that's completely normal because of the way they make their blends. Instead of mixing up a mashbill of corn, wheat, and rye, standard practice in Canada is to mash a wheat whisky, a corn whisky, and a rye whisky and age them separately. After they reach maturity, they are blended together and then blended into the final whisky. Why? Because that's how they've been doing it, and it creates the whisky flavors they need to make the final blend. Some have even more complicated paths, dumping at two years and reblending with other whiskies or more of the same, marrying that into different casks, all of it in the name of flavor consistency.

40 Creek Confederacy Oak

There's rye spice, dark brown sugar, cedar, and pencil points in the nose. But on the palate? It's a swervy blend of rye oil, crusted brown sugar, spicy oak, and figs that really turns my head. Blended? Splendid!

Now add what the Canadians call "flavoring whisky," or the Scots and Irish call "malt whiskey," or the Irish "single pot still whiskey." The Japanese generally blend like the Scots do but may age in plum liqueur casks or Japanese oak. They may also blend with bulk whiskeys purchased from Scotland or Ireland to cover the current acute shortage of Japanese whisky. (My thanks to Japanese whisky writer Brian Ashcraft for explaining Japanese whisky regulations to me!)

It's not all that simple, of course. For example, take the aptly named Jim Beveridge, the master blender for Johnnie Walker. With the full resources of Diageo's twenty-eight malt whisky distilleries and the variety of grain whiskies made at the truly massive Cameronbridge Distillery, Beveridge has a dizzying array of whiskies to work with.

But it may well be that there are other whiskies that go into Johnnie Walker. There's a long-established traditional business agreement known as "reciprocation" that covers distillers trading barrels of whisky with each other for blending purposes. The blender has a wide, wide landscape to work with.

"Every few months, I'd taste it."

Until I started prying into it, I assumed that blending a new whiskey was work completed in a couple weeks.

Surely the blenders knew what the whiskeys tasted like going in; it was just a matter of finding the right proportions and carefully noting how much of which whiskeys went in. Of course, you'd have to consider sustainability and blend with whiskeys you'd have available in the future, but still, we've all mixed beers, mixed cocktails, and mixed whiskeys on the tabletop. How hard could this be?

Then I was talking to the late Dave Pickerell about a bottling of WhistlePig he'd done, I think it was the Old World Rye Madeira Finish. He described trying different ratios of the Madeira finish, Sauternes finish, and port finish—10 ml (0.3 fluid ounce) more or less of one or the other—and I realized that he had taken samples along with him on the road and was blending in his hotel room after a long day of meetings. That's involved. Maybe this takes longer than I thought.

About a year later, Ardbeg flew me (and some other writers) to Islay for the launch of their new An Oa bottling. We were in the

"rounding room," a new facility in the distillery compound where the crucial final step of blending An Oa took place: marrying. An Oa was supposed to be a more accessible version of Ardbeg's powerful peaty character, "the iron fist in a velvet glove," as master blender Dr. Bill Lumsden put it.

He's talking about putting whisky aged in ex-bourbon, ex-PX sherry, and virgin bourbon barrel together, going back and forth with his protégé, Brendan McCarron, about how McCarron had a blend that they thought was right but wasn't quite exactly what they wanted. So Lumsden said, he left the bottle on his desk while they worked on other things.

Then he said the Thing: "Every few months, I'd taste it."

Now, for Lumsden, this is where he realized that what the blend still needed, to become exactly what he wanted in An Oa, was time spent together, because the sample kept getting better. The time would be spent in the rounding room in a vat made from used French oak (more porous, more oxygen transfer). "Marrying isn't often done," he told us. "It's expensive; it's a pain in the ass." But it really brought things together for this blend.

Meanwhile I'm standing there realizing that this blend has taken a year to create. It's a huge job, on top of making their regular bottlings—the Ardbeg 10 and Glenmorangie Original and such—every week, sourcing rare wine barrels, and figuring out new things to do with Glenmorangie (because people expect that). Well, and talking to ignorant journalists, too.

Blending isn't throwing things together in an afternoon. It's hard work, a life's work that you must practice for years to get to the point where you can recognize what's needed to achieve something great.

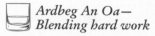

Ardbeg An Oa— Blending hard work

Ardbeg An Oa is a sherry-heavy expression. Wet smoke comes on through dried berries and fresh mulberries. Gobs of malt sweeten up the smoke, which is coming on heavy, and the fruit runs through it all. Well integrated.

"EVERY FEW MONTHS, I'D TASTE IT."

The "gathering vat," at Ardbeg, for making An Oa

The blender has to consider that when three or more whiskeys go together, they may lose parts of themselves, have them masked by components of the other whiskeys. A blender has to know the characteristics of all the whiskeys available at a given time.

Richard Paterson, famed blender of the Dalmore, Jura, and Whyte & MacKay whiskies, says that he approaches blending like a cocktail party and all the whiskies as personalities. Then he puts together the guest list to make an interesting party: some society folk, some artists, an academic or lawyer, a few engineers, and maybe a couple bikers. "And then it's "Hello, how are you?'" he says, straight-faced but with a twinkle in his eye.

Consider also that once a blender has learned what all the available whiskies smell and taste like, and the blender has built a map of what flavors come from what warehouses, the job shifts up a level. The blender has to develop a sense for what every whisky tastes like by smell alone, because tasting 120 whiskies a day, even sips of just 5 ml (0.2 fluid ounce), is a quick path to a numb tongue and a sodden brain, not to mention the long-term health effects. A blender learns what whiskies smell like at 50 percent, 40 percent, 20 percent, and then what they taste like with each of fifty or so different whiskies blended into them.

It's no easy job. But when you learn how to blend in just a hint of smoke; to bring out the blackberry; to blend malt, fruit, sandalwood, and a wisp of bonfire to suggest a forest; or to build a roaring wave of caramel and toast, black pepper and cedar, with a touch of ginger that shows off everything a whisky can be, you've done more than build a whisky. You've built a reputation.

Tasting the Warehouse

A blender often works alone, backed up by a tasting panel that will trial the blends to reach a consensus.

Blenders also rely on the warehouse staff, who have a strong sense for where the best barrels are. In years gone by, that was often because they'd be smelling the barrels and illicitly dipping samples. It's blender's lore that the best barrels in the warehouse are the shiny ones because they're the ones that the warehousemen's coveralls and leather aprons are always rubbing against as they lean in to steal a sip.

Sampling used to involve rolling out barrels, lowering them to have the bungs knocked out, and having a sample dipped out with a siphon-like device known as a "thief." Then the whole thing would be reversed to put the barrel back. These days it's a matter of a quick buzz with a sparkless electric drill into the head of the barrel, catching the spout of whiskey in a sample tube, and pounding a small wooden plug into the hole—a minute's work. The speed allows more samples, and the use of bar codes on every barrel means more accuracy.

The blender (or the distiller in some operations; titles and responsibilities vary) doesn't really sample every barrel, certainly not in large companies. The blender will nose and taste representative samples, and two or three barrels will stand for entire areas of the warehouses. As they develop, the blender will go back and taste them. Over years, the blender will get to know the distinctive areas of the houses and will probably develop favorites.

Booker's, Teresa's Batch, 2019-01

Taste it like a blender: unfiltered, uncut, untouched. Full-bore 62.9 percent bourbon. Hot brown sugar, vanilla, and cinnamon blow out your nose (nothing shy here); all that and hardcore oak on the palate. Booker's isn't just whiskey; it's an experience.

It reminds me of something the late Ronnie Eddins, longtime Buffalo Trace Distillery warehouse manager, told me, about three years before he died. "You know, in your life, you only get about two chances to learn from a 15-year-old bourbon," he said. "There's your first one, and you learn from it all along the time, and you put all that into the second one. By the time the second one's done… you're usually about done, too."

That's why a blender should always be working on another important part of the job: training a successor.

A Drop of the Pure

The blender's work isn't done when the big batches of blended whiskey are made. Blended whiskey is the big seller for Scotch and Irish, Canadian and Japanese.

But single malts, single pot still, and of course bourbon and rye all have to be made; and they're going to take the blender's skill, as well. Even the whiskey that isn't "blended" has to be blended. Unless a whiskey is a single barrel, it's been blended, which can be confusing.

It might help if we had a bigger vocabulary for this topic. No one wants to put the word "blend" on a whiskey that's not of the type we traditionally refer to as "blended." Some distillers try to make the distinction by saying they "mingle" or "marry" the different barrels used to make a whiskey. But in the end, blending is what's being done.

Why is this so? Why can't you just pull barrels of the same age and type and just combine them? Unless you skipped directly to this chapter without reading the rest of the book first, you shouldn't have to ask that. There are so many factors combining to make barrels different that despite everything the distillery manager does to make the whiskey uniform, the blender is still faced with the task of smoothing things out to make

the whiskey consistent before it goes in the bottle. That's why at most distilleries, the person or people who do the blending are considered the most important people on the site.

Blending seems simple, but it's fiendishly difficult when it's done right. It can be a bit opaque to the general drinker. There are some things about whiskey that seem naturally resistant to being understood. Blending is at the heart of a few of them. For instance

1. *The Canadian rule of one-eleventh does not mean that any given bottle is, say, 9 percent prune wine.*

2. *Two bourbons of roughly the same age from the same distiller, with the same mashbill, are not "the same whiskey with a different label/price."*

3. *An 18-year-old single malt (or blend) is not necessarily the same whiskey as the same distillery's 12 year old, just six years older.*

To address these: The Canadian rule says that 9.09 percent (one part in eleven) of a blended whisky can be other alcoholic beverages (that are also aged in wood), but there's nothing that says they *must* be. Make inquiries, check websites, and most importantly, taste them. If you like them, does it really matter?

Bourbons from the same distiller, of the same mashbill, are different because of how long they're aged and where they are aged (except for Four Roses; more on that in a bit). Blanton's bourbon always comes from Warehouse H at Buffalo Trace Distillery, for instance, because it's an ironclad (their other warehouses are stone and brick), which pushes the bourbon into the wood on faster cycles. It makes for a notably different bourbon from Elmer T. Lee, which comes from the middle floors of Warehouses I and K; but they're both made from the same "recipe."

Four Roses has flipped that on its head by employing two mashbills and five yeasts to make ten different bourbons that they take great pains to age separately and consistently in single-story warehouses. They then blend from among those ten whiskeys to make their different bourbons.

What a boring world it would be if single malt whiskey simply ran to a clock. DING! The 12 year old's done. DING! The 15 year old's done. DING! The 21 year old's done. Some are done this way, but other blenders take the opportunity to show off the variety of their whiskeys.

Maybe the 12 year old is all done in first-fill ex-bourbon barrels: round, sweet, dessert flavors of vanilla, coconut, and caramel—soft and easy for the everyday drinker. Now bring up the 15 year old and you're ready to release some of your sherry-casked whiskey, some first-fill and second-fill, adding some spice and fruit to the mix, and a different slant on your distillery character from the 12 year old. Then say the 21 year old is a mix of second-fill barrels, with a little bit of first-fill ex-sherry thrown in. Suddenly you've got a very different whisky indeed—which is exactly what you want from a much older age statement—and a much higher ticket price.

Canadian Club 41 Year Old

Long aging can be a disaster— or a wonder. This is wonderfully lively at forty-one years: cedar, caramel, and sweet fruit aromas, flavors of caramel, toffee, and oaky spice, with that light cedar veneer to it. Striking.

Flavored Whiskey

Let's get this out of the way. I'm not much of a fan of flavored whiskey; there's enough flavor in regular whiskey for me. But I do not look down my nose at anyone who likes the stuff. If that's what you like, well, good on you.

At the very least it's more sales for the whiskey company, and that's always good in the long run.

If you're wondering how the flavor gets in there, it's pretty simple. The whiskey is made, just the way we've been telling you, and then a flavoring is added. It might be an infusion, a syrup, or an essence. If there is additional sugar added, chances are you've made your whiskey into a liqueur or cordial; and if you've diluted the spirit below 40 percent ABV, you'll hit some regulatory barriers to calling it "whiskey" in many countries.

That's really the limit of what I have to say. I'm just here to talk about how flavor gets into whiskey, after all, and this is a straightforward addition. As to whether it's still "whiskey" or not, I'll leave that to the regulators and your personal opinion. Be polite and enjoy yourselves.

Blenders Make the Whiskey

It's no secret that the vast majority of the bottles of whiskey sold every day are branded, regular bottlings that you'll see on the shelf week after week: Jack Daniel's Old No. 7, Glenfiddich 12 Year Old, Jameson, Johnnie Walker Red, Crown Royal, Yamazaki 12 Year Old, and hundreds of others that are standard expressions that distillers and blenders produce year round. They are not the one-off limited releases that might generate wild excitement, but they are the bottles that drinkers and bars buy again and again, without hesitation.

There are "recipes" for blending these flagship and regular offerings. So many barrels of this type, so many of the others, dump and mingle them. Some distillers may allow the whiskeys to "marry" together for as long as a month; some may have them together only long enough to fill the tank that feeds the bottling line.

But before it goes in the bottle, the blending team will sample to make sure the batch meets the guidelines for that expression. If it does, the buttons are pressed and levers are pulled, and the bottles fill. If it's not quite right, it's back to the master, and time for a

tweak; a few more barrels of one parcel or another. It doesn't happen often, but the blend will always come out right. That's the blender's job.

Blending makes the whiskey, really. The blender takes what the farmer, the brewer, the yeast, the barrel, and the warehouse yield and makes whiskey, consistently, with art and individuality.

As I keep saying: horses for courses. The everyday flagship bottle of blended Scotch or 4-year-old bourbon, the delicately balanced 50-year-old single malt, or the deftly resurrected interpretation of a long-gone single pot still recipe—blenders make sense of what is given them, whatever the charge from the head office may be. Even when you're talking about a single-cask bottling, chances are very good that it's the blender picking that cask. Who better?

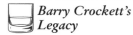 **Barry Crockett's Legacy**

Boy to man, Crockett blended Irish whiskeys. This is his valedictory: a matured version of Redbreast's joyful fruit bowl, deep caramel, and baked desserts, all smooth as oiled glass. A masterpiece.

The Bottle

Chapter 13:

If you've read much about whiskey, you've probably read that whiskey doesn't change once it's bottled. If you *haven't* read that before, I'll tell you now: Whiskey doesn't change once it's bottled—until you open it.

It's not quite true, because if the whiskey's mistreated—set in the sun, subjected to extreme heat or cold, or tilted so the whiskey touches the cork, or if the cork is tainted—it will change the flavor. But under pretty simple optimal conditions (out of direct light, at room temperature or a bit cooler) the flavor of whiskey doesn't change between being bottled and being opened for consumption.

If that's true, then why does a book about how flavor is created in whiskey have a chapter on bottling? That's because even after a whiskey is dumped from the barrel and mingled, blended, or married, there are still some things that can add or change or take away flavor before the whiskey is put in the bottle— and then before the whiskey hits your glass.

Filtering, proofing, coloring, packaging, and transportation may have an effect. Because of the subjective nature of taste, even the shape of the bottle, the name of the whiskey, or the price can affect the flavor of whiskey for individuals. We'll talk about this more in the final chapters, but we're going to touch on it here, when we talk about the sensual experience of opening a bottle of whiskey. First let's get the whiskey in the bottle to begin its trip to your glass.

Filtering

There are a couple different layers of filtering that take place with whiskey once its aged (the charcoal filtering of Tennessee whiskey, the Lincoln County Process, takes place before aging). There is the coarse filtering that takes place when barrels of whiskey are dumped after aging, which is a simple physical screen to catch bits of char from the inside of the barrel. There may be a more restrictive filtration through layered pads to remove more material.

There is another step that can be taken, called chill filtration. There are proteins in whiskey that are in solution. Extreme cold can cause these proteins to denature, to change at a molecular level as some of the weaker molecular bonds break. This will bring them out of solution and cause cloudiness in the whiskey. This chill haze isn't harmful, but it can look like a flaw and can cause consumers to reject the whiskey as a potential purchase.

To avoid this issue, distillers may chill filter their whiskey. This requires chilling the whiskey to 32°F (0°C) or lower, which will cause the haze to form. Then the whiskey is filtered through pads or sheets, and the haze particles are left behind. Potential problem solved; but what about the flavor; that's just been stripped out?

That's a matter of some debate. While there is definitely *something* being filtered out, judging by the smell and somewhat greasy feel of the pads, I understand that blind tasting of filtered and unfiltered whiskeys has been inconclusive.

On the basis of that possibility, though, some distillers have made the decision to avoid chill filtration. That's easy to do, it turns out. If a whiskey is bottled at 46 percent ABV or higher, it prevents the haze from forming. Problem solved, if that's a proof where the whiskey tastes best to you.

Proofing

What does proof have to do with flavor? It's all about water: colorless, odorless, tasteless water.

To hear some people, you might think water is the very worst thing that could happen to whiskey. Whiskey snobs, who will suck the fun out of this fantastic liquid by telling you everything you must or mustn't do to enjoy whiskey, will tell you that the only "right" way to drink whiskey is neat, with no added water and no ice, ever. They may allow a scant few drops of spring water "to open it up," but they'll want to use water from the same source as the distillery and add it with an eyedropper.

I love to watch their heads explode when I point out that during the bottling process, significant amounts of water are added to almost every whiskey (except the cask-strength ones) in the process called "proofing."

The whiskey comes out of the cask at, say, 55 percent ABV; but the bottled product is at 40 percent. The only way that happens is by adding water. It's highly purified water, put through processes like deionization, distillation (how's that for irony?), or reverse osmosis to pull any

possible flavor out of the water so it doesn't affect the flavor of the whiskey. Only, it does. That's part of the reason you see so many different proofs on whiskeys.

"Proof" is an old word for the alcohol strength of a spirit. According to the researchers at Britannica.com, the use of the word goes back to sixteenth-century England. A spirit would be tested ("proofed") for strength by soaking a small charge of gunpowder with the spirit. If the wet gunpowder could be lit, the liquor was deemed to be a "proof spirit" and was taxed at a higher rate.

There were obvious problems with this test. Gunpowder from different mills had different compositions, and the test was affected by temperature; warmer spirits would light more readily. The test was done away with when analytical methods caught up with requirements in 1816. If the specific gravity of the spirit— its relative weight compared to an equal volume of water— corresponded to an alcohol content of at least 57 percent ABV, it was a proof spirit.

The determination of proof is now a relatively straightforward analytical test of alcohol content, usually by volume. Determining what proof a bottling *should* be is a different matter. There are economic reasons, to be sure. Many cynical drinkers have pointed out that lowering the proof results in more whiskey to sell, just by adding water, and sometimes that's the main reason.

There are flavor reasons as well, because proof can directly affect flavor. Distillers consider the use of the whiskey (there's that "horses for courses" thing again) and the market for the whiskey. Is this a whiskey for highballs? For more involved cocktails? Or for neat sipping? Each one may require a different proof.

Look at a shelf of whiskeys. You'll see a lot of whiskeys bottled at 40 percent ABV, mainly because that's the legal low end for whiskey in most countries (and in all of the Big Five whiskey producers). But it's also where you find almost all Canadian whisky, almost all blended Scotch whisky, and where you'll find (since 2004) Jack Daniel's Old No. 7.

It's a popular proof for many whiskey drinkers because many whiskey drinkers like their whiskey as "whiskey and." That's whiskey and water, whiskey and ginger ale, whiskey and cola, whiskey and juice, even the humble whiskey on the rocks. They want the flavor of whiskey in a refreshing drink, nothing more. I enjoy a highball myself and usually reach for something in the low 40 percent range to make it. Much more and the whiskey is going to overwhelm the drink.

You can also enjoy a good blended whiskey at 40 percent all by itself for the same reason. Too much alcohol can punch away the flavors of the whiskey, heat up the aromas, light up the finish with a blaze of perceived heat. The lower-proof blends make a great everyday whiskey because of this.

Let's keep looking at our shelf; 40 percent isn't the only proof. It goes up incrementally starting at a simple 40.5 percent and running up to the low 70 percent region for a couple exceptionally strong bottlings, for a variety of reasons.

The high-proof bottlings embody a simply understood desire to deliver the whiskey right from the barrel. As the late Booker Noe said of his eponymous Booker's bottling, the whiskey is uncut— no proofing water added—and unfiltered, the way the distillers and blenders (and warehouse workers, on the sly) taste them. These cask strength/barrel proof whiskeys have every bit of flavor that's in the barrel. They also have every bit of alcohol fire, but drinkers can tame that by adding water to just the right level for their own individual tastes.

An example of some DIY proofing

In between the low and high end of the range is where proofing gets interesting. Think about the reasons for adding water to your glass of whiskey and you'll get a peek into the thinking of the blenders and distillers who add water to their bottles. The neat freaks are right; you add water to a whiskey to open it up. But how does that work?

Adding water changes the alcohol level, which changes the aromas that come forward. More alcohol will carry oak tones; lower the alcohol and the oak backs down, allowing the richer vanilla notes to come out. Distillers will proof whiskeys to different levels to find the optimum aroma profile or to find the level that brings out the particular flavor they're looking for.

Adding water doesn't change what flavor components are in a whiskey, nor does it take them away or add them. Adding water changes how whiskey presents itself to your senses, shifts what you sense first or more intensely. It's like a person changing her wardrobe. The person is the same, but your perception of them is different.

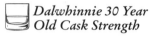 ### Dalwhinnie 30 Year Old Cask Strength

At 56.4 percent, the nose is tight malt and white balsamic vinegar; tastes of dry oak and digestive biscuit. Add water: Honey and crusty bread aromas, and a generous mouth of honeyed malt and lighter, spicier oak. Just add water.

Age in the Bottle

I get this question all the time. "I have a bottle of Old Riverboat 12-year-old rye whiskey from 1965. That's 12 plus 55 years old, so this is a 67 year old whiskey, right?" No, it's a 55-year-old bottle of 12-year-old whiskey.

While there are some changes that take place in a bottle, very slowly over many years, generally speaking, as long as the seal is intact and no large amount of evaporation is taking place, whiskey doesn't change in the bottle until it is opened. Whiskey needs either wood or oxygen to change flavor at that point, and there is a small amount of oxygen in a sealed bottle. But if you're not shaking the bottle, it's going to be a very slow and limited interaction.

Once you open the bottle, all bets are off. I have what I call a "forty and out" rule. Once I get down to about 40 percent of the whiskey left in the bottle, I figure on finishing it within six months. Otherwise it's going to be robbed of its liveliness. Drink up; whiskey's wasting.

Darker doesn't always mean more time in the barrel.

Coloring

Some whiskeys are allowed to have added coloring; some are not. It's a matter of the laws of the countries where they are made.

American whiskeys are generally not allowed to have added coloring under the federal "standards of identity" (there are some exceptions made for blended whiskeys). Scotch, Irish, Japanese, and Canadian whiskeys are allowed to add color. Other countries vary.

This is generally limited to the addition of what's called "spirit caramel." Caramel is sugar that has been heated until it browns, which can then be used to color or *flavor* other foods or liquids. The argument for using spirit caramel has always been to allow the creation of a consistent color for an expression of whiskey, given the natural variation of color uptake from barrels. Some batches may be lighter or darker than others and may wind up on shelves next to each other, which would be disconcerting to the customer. A judicious addition of caramel is made to reach a consistent color.

Some drinkers question when caramel is used for consistency, and when a dose of caramel might be used, consistently, to darken an expression's color, suggesting that the whiskey might be older than it is (longer time in the barrel often makes for a darker whiskey). There's not really a way to know, though it's pretty easy to be suspicious. Some distillers (and some independent bottlers) have made a point of not adding caramel to any of their whiskeys, presumably in the name of transparency of motive.

But our question is whether the addition of caramel for color affects the flavor. Opinions vary, as opinions do. It doesn't take much caramel to affect color, but caramel's flavor could easily hide against the sweet background flavor of whiskey. Perhaps it boosts that sweetness; perhaps it boosts the nutty character of the grains. Or perhaps it doesn't. It's likely subtle and subjective, but it's something to be aware of as a possible factor in the flavor of, let's say, curiously dark whiskeys aged in used barrels.

The Bottle on the Shelf

This last section is also somewhat subjective, though not entirely. The most subjective part is the effect of the packaging—the bottle shape and heft, the look of the label and the bottle closure, and any box or tube the bottle comes in—on your perceived impression of the whiskey's flavor.

Somewhat less subjective are any negative effects of transporting the whiskey and how it is stored. I know I've seen many bottles sitting on shelves in front of windows, subjected to bright sunlight for hours every day. I've read about bottles being stored in unventilated containers in the summer. You may have seen this yourself and wondered what that was doing to the whiskey.

Briefly, heat and light are bad for whiskey, but light is worse by far. Direct light from the Sun or electric lights can cause flavor compounds in the whiskey to break down into smaller components. It also works on the molecules of color. Leave a whiskey in sunlight for a year or so, and you can be left with a substantially paler and significantly different tasting spirit.

Heat seems to mostly shift the flavor of whiskey slightly in the direction of sweeter, richer. But if a whiskey bottle gets too hot, the alcohol could start to vaporize, and the resulting pressure inside the bottle could break the seal. Then the alcohol vapor escapes, and that's what makes open whiskey change flavor.

I had this happen once on an unexpectedly hot summer day. I was driving to a whiskey tasting out on Long Island from my Pennsylvania home and went to air-conditioning as the temperature climbed almost to 100°F (37.8°C). About 20 miles (32.2 km) east of Brooklyn, I started smelling whiskey. I stopped and found that a new bottle of whiskey had popped its cork, right through the shrink-wrapped plastic cover.

From then on, I took care to always keep whiskey out of direct sunlight.

That's the kind of thing that could happen to a whiskey on even a relatively short trip from a wholesaler's warehouse to a bar, or from a store to your home. It doesn't hurt to take a moment to sniff around the seal of a new bottle. If you smell a noticeable aroma of whiskey, you probably want to leave that one alone on the chance that the seal's been compromised.

On a more subjective note, a fancy or heavy bottle can lead to expectations of quality that will color your perception of a whiskey's flavor. That's human nature and the distillers certainly know that.

Think about picking up a new bottle of whiskey. Consider hefting a whiskey with a very plain label, a lightweight and generic-shape bottle, and then twisting open a plastic screw top. Now, weigh a heavy-based bottle in your hand, feel the richly embossed label with a history of the distillery and details of the composition of the whiskey, and peel open the lead foil capsule around a cork-and-wood closure. You'll expect more from the second bottle, no matter what's inside it. As a friend of mine said about an expensive bottle we opened, "Of course it's going to taste great. At that price, it has to!"

We'll talk more about that later. For now, remember that it's part of the effect, and it's as real as gravity when you're drinking, and it's completely a nonfactor when you're doing a blind tasting.

Finally what happens to the flavor of a whiskey when you do open it? Oxygen gets at the whiskey as soon as the seal is broken and really attacks the whiskey when you start to pour it and the liquid is agitated.

Is that all bad? Sometimes a whiskey will actually taste better, more complex, when a bit of aeration takes place. There are pouring devices that increase that aeration, forcing oxygen into the whiskey. Oxygenation is at the heart of most accelerated aging schemes, so there's definitely an effect.

Any positive effects of added oxygen, though, are pretty short lived before loss of alcohol starts the inevitable downhill slide. As alcohol vapor escapes every time the bottle is opened, your whiskey will taste a bit dull, without the lively notes of fruit and flowers that delighted you. It will taste less and less special, becoming a pale reminder of what it once was. This will take some months in a closed bottle, given normal conditions.

You can slow this process even more in a couple ways. The easiest is to use the same preservative gases that wine drinkers use to preserve an open bottle of wine. A quick puff of a spray can before closing the bottle tightly can help preserve the flavor. You can also carefully and slowly decant a half-full bottle to a smaller bottle so as to store the whiskey with less "headspace" and oxygen.

Eventually, though, as mentioned in the sidebar, you'll want to get down to the business of finishing that bottle while it still tastes great. Don't be in a rush, but do your whiskey a favor and say goodbye to it when it's still close to its best. That way, you'll have nothing but great memories of a great bottle, which is how all whiskeys should leave this world.

The People

Chapter 14:

I like to say that there's one important ingredient in making good whiskey that's crucial but hard to quantify. There's the grain, the yeast, the water, the still, the barrel and the time in it, and the climate. But there's something else that's so important that we often overlook it. That's the will, the intent, and the purpose of the people making the whiskey.

It's not just the brewers, distillers, blenders, and warehouse workers, either. It's everyone: the farmers and maltsters, the sawyers and coopers, the people who plan and build the warehouses. It may even include people whose influence continues after their retirement or death.

It includes the people in the chain who get that whiskey from the barrel to your palate as well: people like the bottlers and the folks who design those bottles and their packages. There are the marketers who decide it's time for a new bottling, the blenders and distillers who design and create it, and the sales staff who then get out there and buttonhole bar managers and store buyers. They in turn put it in front of you, and the brand ambassador may come along and awake a thirst for that whiskey in you.

Take away any of those people, take away their drive and execution, and that whiskey may never reach your tongue. That's important, very important stuff indeed. Let's have a close look at what these people do and how they advance the taste of whiskey till it lands where it needs to be.

Jimmy and Eddie Russell, father and son master distillers at Wild Turkey Distillery

Seeds

Whiskey starts with grain, and grain grows on a farm. There is more than one type of farmer who raises grain for whiskey. Some operate the big farms that raise tons and tons of grain. They plant and tend fields that are 0.5 mile (0.8 km) on a side, planting and harvesting with huge specialized machines.

Farming for them is about clean yield per acre, and they're very good at it. An Iowa farmer counts on a yield of over 200 bushels of corn (over 11,000 pounds [4989.5 kg]) per acre of ground. Scottish farmers will get about two and a half tons (2268 kg) of barley from an acre, and 30 percent of the national crop will go to the distilling and brewing industries. The consistency of their crop makes the distillers' jobs easier and helps make the whiskey consistent.

There are the farmers who are growing smaller fields of specialized crops, maybe to organic or non-GMO standards. They may be "salt of the earth" types who do things the old way, with natural fertilizers, contour plowing, and forty-year-old tractors. They may be new-tech farmers, using Bluetooth-enabled moisture probes in every field to keep tabs on the crops, maybe even

in individual rows. They are farmers who are willing to take a risk to produce something other than commodity grains. They're filling a precise need some distillers have for a "clean" grain that allows them to make a whiskey they can present as less processed, more natural than others. They may even be the distillers themselves, growing the grain to make their whiskey.

There are also farmers like Robert McDonald at Dancing Star Farms in Imler, Pennsylvania, who grows more than ten varieties of corn for seed, including Bloody Butcher, Wapsie Valley, Blue Dent, and Cocke's Prolific. He's growing for other farmers and working with distillers directly to make those relationships. I ran into him at the Pennsylvania Whiskey Convention not long ago, and he was very happy with the response he was getting from the small distillers.

There are farmers who very much want to try farming like this, being able to make money with grain crops that aren't for everyone. This is what the farmer-distiller relationship looks like today. Small distillers want boosted, different flavor; and they're willing to pay a premium for it.

Maltsters also work with the distillers. Forty years ago, it was just come to work, clean the seed, and make ton after ton of pale malt. As the market has changed, as the character of whiskey has changed, maltsters are reacting to market demands and trying to anticipate them.

The interesting thing for me here is that while there are small maltsters starting up in a variety of places, offering various custom services, there are also moves by the very large maltsters to meet these needs. I recently visited the huge Great Western maltings in Vancouver, Washington, eighty years old and so big we had to drive around it. They were serving the craft brewing and distilling industries at this immense place, making thirty-five different varieties of malt and working on new ideas in a very advanced pilot plant on-site. They're eager to find new flavors from grain.

Up the coast from that Great Western facility, there's a new company where they're changing the way malting is done. Skagit Valley Maltings grew from local engineers breadboarding an all-in-one-vessel malting system in response to the local farmers growing nonstandard barley varieties. The accepted commodity barley strains didn't grow well in the area, but heirloom and newer hybrid strains did. The problem was that no big maltings wanted to run those grains through their plants. The answer was local malting, and the company is growing fast to meet demand from distillers and brewers for more flavorful malt.

These people are making a difference in the flavor and character of new whiskeys. The farmers in Scotland who annually buck the system at the request of some distillers and grow Golden Promise, Maris Otter, Minstrel, or other, older strains of barley that have fallen out of favor help make that difference. Without their will to do something different, whiskeys would taste more and more alike.

Wood

I once went out in the Missouri woods with a sawyer and his crew (and Buffalo Trace Distillery master distiller Harlen Wheatley, who actually cut down an oak tree that day). It was hot, felling the tree involved a chainsaw technique that went dead against everything I'd been taught about safety.

When I got back, I found six ticks crawling around on me. Going out and cutting down oak trees to make barrels takes the right kind of person. They also know what they're doing. These days, sawyers are cutting only the right oaks for barrels because they know the inspectors at the mills are only going to pay for the right ones. They have to be straight, 16 to 22 inches (40.6 to 55.9 cm) in diameter with no branches for the first 20 feet (6.1 m), about 80 to 100 years old, and it's preferred that they be from northern-facing slopes.

Cut the right trees and you get the right wood for barrels, barrels that make whiskey with consistent character. Cut too many out of one area and the character of the barrels could shift as trees have to be harvested from nonoptimal areas or simply from areas where the flavors that come from the wood will be different. These are long-view decisions, and it likely helps that many of the small companies that do the logging for barrel making are family concerns.

The sawyer makes that decision, and the wood moves on to the mill. The workers at the mill mainly do a piece-by-piece job, and they do it well, aided by automation, laser-tracked saws, and video inspection. Their job is to make sure the wood is the same every time. The engineers who work with them may find new ways to cut the wood, make it come together more tightly, change the loss rate, and change how the whiskey matures. Chemists and tree scientists track the changes in oak caused by the length of time the wood is left out to season and dry, and what changes are brought by kilning. These days, there are always experiments going on to see what treatment makes a difference in flavor, retention, and cost.

The coopers who make the barrels are a fascinating cross of traditionalist keepers of the flame and laser-guided innovationists. They raise a barrel by eye and hand, they cut the wood with automated precision, and they hammer it into shape with a practiced skill.

We know that barrels impart a large amount of flavor to whiskey. The people in the labs at the cooperages work with the distilleries and experiment with the wood to find new ways to treat it, heat it, toast it, or char it to make a difference in that flavor.

Some of it is more physical. Brown-Forman makes their Coopers' Craft bourbon with a special coopering technique they call "chiseling" that leaves a series of grooves in the inside of the charred barrel. The wood that is chiseled out is left in the barrel.

All of this is designed to get more surface contact with the wood and spirit. This is just the latest in a series of experiments over the years: cuts, saw-toothed staves, heavier charring.

People in many places are thinking every day about ways to work with wood—before it even touches the whiskey—that will get more flavor into the bottle, with different character.

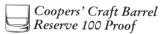 *Coopers' Craft Barrel Reserve 100 Proof*

Grooves are chiseled in the barrel interior, and the wood shavings are left in for extra surface area. Bold oak and char aromas on a 100° proof heat wave; crisp Asian pear frames marshmallow and caramel; oak fires the finish.

Techs

Experiments bring data to mind, and the people who collect and track data have made a difference in whiskey and how it tastes in the same way they've made a difference in almost every industry.

The whiskey industry, in general, used to just move along, doing things as they'd always done. "Don't change a damned thing" is a watchword in the business (and the literal advice given to John Lunn by retired distiller Ralph Dupps when Lunn took the reins at the George Dickel distillery).

There were exceptions and innovators, especially as new materials and technologies were developed. But computers led to an explosive number of changes, with easier and more certain ways of tracking the results of process changes. For instance, millions and millions of barrels of whiskey move through hundreds of warehouses around the globe, and almost every one of them is tracked from fill to dump (and refill and dump and so on), thanks to bar codes and data recording.

That was just the beginning in wood science. Dendrochronologists studied the growth rings on the best barrels to see how the trees had grown. Sawyers and foresters were recruited to track the position of each tree felled: hill, valley, north or south facing, boggy or sandy soil. Chemical analysis of cut wood as it seasoned showed changes in structure and flavor precursors. Probes in the barrels tracked temperature and pressure of the aging whiskey over months and years. The results of wood treatments, different warehouse positions, and seasonal variations all come together in easily consulted records; and decisions are made.

Process has become more transparent. Temperatures of distillation, length of cook, time of fermentation, yeast cell counts, alcohol levels—every bit of data that can be recorded is becoming digitized. Once those data points are connected to sensory evaluations done by trained tasters and chemical testing done in the labs, changes in flavor can be tracked to changes in process.

Data is then applied back to those processes in the form of automation. Track all the still runs in a year and you'll find the best ones. Then a programmer writes a series of instructions for automated valves and probes to follow, and you can have the best run every time. You'll know where a tweak will make a difference or not.

Conversely some distillers deliberately choose not to automate. Dickel, to go back there, is the most determinedly nonautomated large distillery I've ever seen, where every operation is done by hand, valves turned by people who are right there, not pushing a button somewhere else. There is a concern that if the process is overly automated, the distillery will eventually be run by people who don't actually understand what it is they're doing, and why—and that could lead to an industry literally on autopilot.

I find romance in this notion, and I believe in the value of variance. The industry needs this kind of multipath approach to making whiskey to provide the variety drinkers want. So long as there are distilleries with equipment that has been in place for fifty years, and sometimes longer, I believe we will see hands-on distillers making whiskey.

Forgiven

In 2013, Wild Turkey Distilling Company released a blend of roughly three parts 6-year-old bourbon and one part 4-year-old rye. The blend was called "Forgiven," and the story was that distillery workers accidentally mixed the two whiskeys together.

Someone was going to get fired, until master distiller Eddie Russell tasted the mix and decided that it was more than good enough to sell. That's the story, anyway, and Eddie swears it's true.

It's not the only change in whiskey flavor that came about because of an accident, chance, or unintended consequences. Single pot still Irish whiskey came about because of a malt tax. Distillers looked to beat it by substituting unmalted barley for part of the recipe. Not only did they save money, but they discovered a delicious new type of whiskey.

Scotch whisky went through a tremendous surge in growth in the second half of the nineteenth century. It seemed as if anyone who could scrape together enough money to build a stone shed big enough to hold two stills was opening a distillery. Some of those eager entrepreneurs bought used stills sight unseen and found that they didn't fit the space they had. So they modified them to wedge them in and, in doing so, radically changed the still geometry and the consequent taste of the spirit.

Some things just happen. It might be by accident; it might be desperation; it might be a reaction to an outside force. The ones that don't work out, well, we probably don't hear about them. The ones that do become part of the lore, and flavor, of whiskey.

The coming of the technicians to the industry may seem to be creating whiskey without the human touch, a reduction of whiskey to numbers. But when the passion of a whiskey lover is combined with the techniques of a data cruncher, great things can happen. Data collection and retrieval systems, and the people who created and adapted those systems, who first saw the utility of them, have made an immense impact on the flavor of whiskey over the past forty years. The workers' contribution has not gone away. It is, if anything, amplified by data collection, which makes ever-finer adjustments possible.

The Makers

Whiskey making is still largely an industry that relies on human senses to measure process.

The mill operator runs the mill to the accepted standards, but the operator still checks the grist for consistency, heat, and smell. A brewer may measure temperature and saccharification to see if fermentation is complete, but the brewer also checks on the bubbles and smell to know how it's progressing and when it's done.

The distiller relies on smell and taste to know when things are right with the cuts, and on sound to know the system is running smoothly. "You can't sneak up on a stillman," I've been told. "They hear anything that's out of place." Warehouse workers, the folks who move and check the barrels, can always tell you where the good barrels are because they know the smell of the different parts of the warehouses.

"Watch Your Bunghole!"

The warehouse workers have a job that combines strength, control, and a quick eye for distances.

They steer the 500-pound (226.8 kg) barrels off the lifts and down the aisles of the warehouses, spinning and stopping them on a dime. That's part of the amazing utility of the modern barrel; one person can easily handle and move 500 pounds (226.8 kg) of freight, stop it, start it, spin it, and turn it.

The trick of the warehouse worker's job is "clocking" the barrels. That's rolling each barrel so that as it comes up against the last barrel in, the bunghole is at the top of the barrel. You don't want the poplar bung touching the whiskey. It's not oak and it's slightly porous.

Say the first barrel into the rack rolls two and a half times to have the bung up; the barrel roller has to position the bung on the bottom of the barrel as they start the roll into the rack. But the next barrel needs to roll less, about a quarter turn less, but not exactly.

It's difficult and what makes it worse is going into the rack and wrestling a 500-pound (226.8 kg) barrel to fix it.

Once a year, the warehouse men and women show off their skills. The Barrel Relay at the Kentucky Bourbon Festival is the high point of the weeklong festival for the distillers. There are individual races and team races, with male and female teams. The barrels have to be rolled on a course that includes three 90-degree turns and then rolled into a rack.

But it's not just how long you take to get them in the rack. For every barrel that's clocked correctly, time is taken off the competitor's elapsed total. The focus on getting the bung topmost on every barrel leads to friends and family hollering, "Watch your bunghole!" It's a fun time, and the winners get bragging rights for the year.

The people who do these jobs are largely maintaining the whiskey. They keep it on track; they know how things are supposed to smell, sound, feel, and taste; and they can stop it before things go off course. These are important jobs, but they're not making new flavors. If they are, after all, they're probably not doing their jobs right.

The people who create new whiskeys are a smaller, heavily trained and experienced group. Credit must be given to the folks who often start the process, a group that is more often blamed than credited: the marketers, the folks in the offices (or sometimes out in the bars and stores, gathering information). They gauge the public taste, they look at the sales of current whiskeys against the stock of barrels needed to make those expressions, and they come up with an idea of how a whiskey should taste.

That's a particularly hard job these days, thanks to people like you and me. Maybe twenty-five years ago, the job was hard because there were stocks of aging whiskey that had to be bottled before they got too old and became undrinkable, or simply evaporated away to nothing. Then people like me and my colleagues helped get people like you and your friends excited about whiskey, and pretty soon the problem was that the stocks of aged whiskey were getting too low to make all the whiskeys we liked and could afford. Bottles got

scarcer, prices went up, and marketers were called.

The marketers and their ilk dream up new whiskeys that the times call for, in their best estimation. We may like the whiskeys or not, but the marketers often have the first call on what they should be. After that, it is up to the other folks in this group—the master distillers, distillery managers, warehouse managers, and blenders—to make that concept into a whiskey, if possible. (In truth, all of these people, at different distilleries and whiskey companies, have had ideas for whiskeys that made it to the shelf.)

The distillers and distillery managers know what is possible with their whiskeys, with their physical plant, and with the barrels they can acquire. Their knowledge guides new projects over years of time as they experiment with new techniques, new mash formulations, new distilling paths, and new types of barrels. A different way of running a still can produce new make with a very different character, ready to age and blend with the standard make. Add a new grain to the mash, or a new peating level, or blend different yeasts, and you've got a new whiskey. One of the most far-reaching decisions can be where to build a warehouse and of what design. Whiskeys may age there over the course of 200 years or more, with a definite influence on the flavor every day.

The warehouse managers would likely know if a new whiskey is possible immediately. They have their fingers on the flow of barrels in and out of every warehouse used for aging. The cliché that "at least 50 percent of the flavor comes from the barrel" tacitly acknowledges that part of that fraction isn't just the individual barrel; it's the warehouse microclimate where it ages. Most of the barrels in America are quite similar—new, charred white oak—but where they are aged can make an enormous difference.

Ryan Maloney of Julio's Liquors (Westborough, MA)

The job of the warehouse manager in a large, varied Scotch distillery is simply mind boggling. Even if the warehouse manager is pulling together only a new single malt, there may be different-sized bourbon barrels, sherry casks, port pipes, Madeira drums, rum casks—all in first-fill or refill. Add the variety of a blended whisky or blended malt, and the possibilities multiply quickly. The warehouse manager's job is to know where everything is and in what condition of aging, and that knowledge is crucial to the blender's job.

The blender has enormous potential effect on a whiskey's flavor. Even given a profile by the people in marketing, it's the blender's job to make that happen or to change it subtly to make it possible. An experienced blender knows all the potential flavor components of a distillery—often more than one distillery—and can pull together barrels to make whiskeys of different character and texture and perceptions of freshness or age. The silly little dabbling I've done in blending has made clear to me how difficult this job is.

When a blender is in place for decades, he has a deeply personal effect on a whiskey brand's shape and overall character. David Stewart, the malt master at William Grant & Sons for more than forty years, has shaped the flavor of Glenfiddich and the Balvenie and made them hugely popular. Richard Paterson has had similar effects on the Dalmore with his love for particular sherry casks. Barry Crockett's sense of

Irish whiskey and the single pot still type has had a profound effect on the entire range at Irish Distillers. Dr. Don Livermore is clearly on a path to similar influence at J. P. Wiser's. Parker Beam carved out a flavor profile for Heaven Hill's whiskeys that will last long after his death in 2017.

The people who make the whiskey make the flavor. They defend that flavor from random effects, they aim it at a consistent target, and when the decision is made to create a new whiskey, they have the tools to do so readily at hand. They are the core team for flavor creation.

Parker's Heritage Blend of Mashbills 2012

A blend of rye and wheat mashbill bourbons. A nose that's sweet, somewhat floral, but not hot, even over 65 percent ABV. Lean and leathery, sweet in reserve, and miles of finish. Indelibly Parker Beam's palate.

Flavor Delivery

The people who actually make the whiskey have an enormous effect on the flavor, of course. Not by semantic twisting either: "They make all the flavor; they make the whiskey!"

I won't kid you. Once the whiskey is dumped, blended, vatted, and proofed, it's going into a bottle and flavor creation is done. No matter how good the bottle looks, how it's presented to you, how you learn the whiskey's story, the flavor is set.

Mostly. Because flavor is always subjective. I've had the same single malt, from the exact same bottle, in two different settings taste significantly different. It was a combination of temperature, weather, ambient aromas, and probably the company. One setting brought the whisky's sherry cask aging surging to the fore, while the other boosted my awareness of the brine and peat.

We are humans, tasting what we feel in the moment. We are "the meat in the machine," as that stillman at the Dalmore referred to himself during a discussion of the relative merits of automation.

So our sensations of taste and pleasure can be influenced by other factors than the pure organoleptic. Try to deny this and you will, I believe, deny yourself some of the pleasures of this very human drink, this truly human accomplishment. Save the denial for tasting whiskey in a blank-white cubicle, from a blue glass, with pen in hand and silent concentration your only companion. At other times, why not taste what comes across your tongue and thus your brain?

Then the people who design the package, the bottle, the label, any kind of presentation box the bottle comes in, can have an effect on your whiskey's taste. If we're going to be honest, probably the people who set the whiskey's price have an effect as well. The reviewer whose opinions you read can affect your experience. The bartender or shop seller may tell you things about the whiskey that will set your expectations in one direction or another; they may even show you an entirely new way to imagine your whiskey. That's happened to me, and I spent hours talking to them and learning as we went.

A brand ambassador may lead you to expect to taste history in the glass or Sun-warmed grain or the crashing waves of a seaside warehouse. This person might take you through a tasting of several whiskeys, guiding your perception at each sip. It's done to sell whiskey, of course. But every brand ambassador I've ever met—and I have a large box full of their cards—has been a true whiskey lover as well, and they most often sincerely want to share that passion and make you a whiskey lover, too.

Even the sales representative you've never met or the store buyer you may never see have had an effect on how the whiskey tastes. After all, if the whiskey isn't there on the shelf, being poured at the bar, because the representative didn't make the sale, it doesn't have any flavor at all!

Whiskey doesn't just happen. The people involved in the process of whiskey making— every one of them—are crucial to the flavor of the whiskey in your glass. At some point in the process, sometimes as the whiskey's being made, sometimes years before, people make decisions and the flavor of the whiskey changes. It might be huge; it might be as light as a bee's wing. But you can taste their decisions there in your glass. Think about them the next time you enjoy a drink.

The Intangibles

There are, I'm sure, people who'd rather see this chapter titled "Nonsense," "Make Believe," or maybe even "Bullshit." This is a chapter about the final additions that add or subtract flavor in whiskey—the ones that are not quantifiable. Any scientist will tell you that if you can't measure it or record it, it didn't happen.

But it isn't scientists who blend whiskeys; or if they do, they don't do it with high-performance liquid chromatography or a mass spectrometer. Whiskey is blended by hand and nose, by palate and memory, by the human perception of the blender. It can be measured using these tools, but it can't be duplicated. Not yet, anyway.

Once a whiskey is made, blended, and bottled, there's still no definitive set of numbers or words about how it tastes. That's because there are few things that are more subjective. We even have a saying about it that goes back to Roman times: "*De gustibus non disputandum est.*" It literally means "taste should not be disputed/discussed." These days, we say, "There's no accounting for taste." You can see this played out on any given day in various online whiskey discussion forums, where if one person praises a whiskey, inevitably another will say that it is garbage and vice versa.

What makes this so? Much of it is personal taste, developed in many curious, even eccentric ways. I didn't drink Old Forester for years because it was the first whisky I ever tried, and at age 11 it simply shocked me. I avoided "that rotten Old Forester" thereafter. Then I tried it again, at the urging of another writer, and I felt like a fool for all the years of drinking a good whisky I'd wasted. It's hard to say how taste develops.

So personal taste, what whiskey you like and don't, is *by definition* intangible. It cannot be touched or truly explained. If that's so, what's hard to believe about flavors coming from intangible sources?

Keep an open mind and let's dive into the waters— Are they murky? Are they clear? Are they even there?—of the Intangibles.

Terroir

Let's start with something that's more than a bit controversial, even in the realm of wine, where it originates.

Terroir is a concept from winemaking, the idea that the very place where the grapes are grown affects the flavor of the wine. The soil, the terrain and topography, the latitude and climate, prevailing winds, perhaps even the local flora and fauna are all included.

Quantifying that is difficult, even with wine, and that's why it's such a controversial concept in whiskey making, which is more process oriented and includes more steps. If it's about where the ingredient is grown, most distillers don't use grain that is grown adjacent to them, or even within 10 miles (16.1 km). Some do, but not most. They may buy from "local" growers or in-state growers, but then which terroir is it?

Is it only about where the grain is grown? Whiskey is certainly an expression of the grain (or grains), but also the wood of the barrel and, quite arguably, the warehouse as well. As we discussed in chapter 9, the type of oak and where it grows has a definite effect on the flavor of the whiskey. Whiskey ages in oak for

quite a bit longer than wine, which is only in the wood for one or two years; so consideration of the oak's origins is reasonable. The warehouse's siting and surrounding terrain make for yet another consideration, affecting the barrels' heating cycle.

It gets more interesting when you consider the differences between the French winemaker's understanding of terroir versus the American winemaker's. The French include regional traditions that have established themselves over decades and centuries: the natural yeasts on the grapes (and in the bellies of the wasps that help pollinate the vines), the way the vines grow. Americans tend to a stricter interpretation: only what is natural, nothing that is man-made or changed by the hands of humans.

Some in the industry, who seem to hew more to the American idea, say that there is no terroir in whiskey. Whiskey is more man-made, more processed than wine is. Grain is malted, milled, hydrated, and cooked. It is then chilled, strained (or not), and fermented with carefully tended yeasts, after which it is subjected to distillation—eliminating all but the higher volatiles—and long aging. How could any influence of the soil be there?

Others disagree, arguing that despite the different natures of wine and whiskey, there is a difference in whiskeys that comes down to locality: the same "taste of the earth" that winemakers talk about. Perhaps, because of that difference between wine and whiskey, there should be a different term for the local effects on flavor in whiskey. Maybe it isn't so much that there is no terroir as it is that we don't discern that effect, because until very recently, most whiskey makers in the modern era were too big to discretely express the kinds of microeffects that terroir represents.

The late distiller Dave Pickerell, a man who kept a famously open mind about possible influences on whiskey flavor, was convinced that the rye grown in the fields around Hillrock Estate Distillery, in New York's Hudson Valley, lent a noticeable difference in flavor to the distillate. He believed that we were only at the beginning of recognizing such microdifferences, thanks to small batch distilling. He was also hoping to discover more differences that might be possible from using locally harvested peat for smoking the malt on site.

I don't have an answer, nor do I have a suggested term for the combination of local effects on grain, oak, and warehouses that may or may not comprise "whiskey terroir." That's why we're in the chapter called "The Intangibles," after all. But it is an intriguing and promising path for craft distillers to investigate.

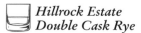 ### *Hillrock Estate Double Cask Rye*

Made from rye grown organically on the distillery farm. Rye dominates: Cinnamon-spiked mint candy on the nose, youthfully oily rye bursts on the tongue, supported by oak-borne vanilla. Distiller Dave Pickerell said this rye had a special minty character from these fields.

Age and Youth

As I grow older, I have to deal with young writers always nipping at my heels (I don't, actually, but it works with the narrative—humor me).

When they do, I remind myself that earned experience trumps youthful exuberance. It does, sometimes. That is why when I want a simply perfect beer, I head for Prague, Brussels, or Bavaria, and when I want a whiskey that's going to be zeroed in on my palate from the first sip, it's going to be from a distillery that's been operating for at least fifty years. No surprises, please.

There is a lot to be said for experience and consistency, especially when it's employed in the service of making top-notch whiskey. Sometimes it gets hijacked into a situation where it's used to make vast quantities of crashingly mediocre stuff, all of which has its place and market niche. But when you look at the whiskey shelves in even a moderately good spirits retailer, there are always some whiskeys there that you know, without hesitation, are 100 percent going to satisfy your desire for a glass of amber glory.

The Big Five whiskey regions are thick with this kind of experience. There are people working at most distilleries who've been there longer than you've been drinking whiskey. I'm no spring chicken, yet there are one or two people who've been working in the industry longer than I've been *alive*. That kind of institutional memory and depth of experience has an effect on a whiskey's flavor that can't be expressed as anything more exciting than "consistent," unless you want to crank it all the way up to "perfect." Don't, though, because the best of these people know that there's always room to make it, as one distiller said to me with a wink, "perfecter."

Does that mean that the craft distillers are all behind the curve until they're fifty years old? Most definitely not. For one thing, some of the craft distillers lured those experienced folks out of retirement or across the street to their operations. Dave Pickerell, mentioned earlier, was the master distiller at Maker's Mark, then started a new career as a consulting distiller and started quite a few new outfits on the path to deliciousness. Jim McEwan continues to escape his retirement from Scotch whisky after long careers at both Bowmore Distillery and Bruichladdich Distillery, either one of which would have established him as a master.

Wyoming Barrel Strength Bourbon

The distilling experience of Bourbon Hall of Famer Steve Nally and master blender Nancy Fraley got this start-up sailing. A king bourbon nose: warehouse, corn, and oak. Both lively and solid on the tongue, minty and corn solid, framed in full-sized oak.

For another, well, it's the same tack as the craft brewers take. Why do things the same way as they've always been done? If they're just making bourbon or just making malt whiskey or just making single pot still and doing it the same way as the established distillers, they can't win. Even if they do it just as well—which is hard because of the experience gulf noted above—it's going to be almost impossible to do it for the same price: economies of scale, lower cost of capital for known businesses, and lower capital debt to begin with.

The smart thing to do is to be different, which is where that youthful exuberance comes in. Some of the stuff I've talked about in other chapters—types of stills, innovative or even crazy mashbills, wild yeasts, different barrels, and heritage grains—are all the result of someone saying, "Wait, I've never seen this before; how about we try this?"

That's about what Christopher Williams, the manager of Coppersea Distilling near Hyde Park, New York, told me about a green malt whiskey they made. "We found an old Scottish distilling text… that mentioned making whiskey from unkilned, fresh malt; you grind it to a paste in a meat grinder. They essentially said 'Don't do this; it's delicious, but it's really difficult.' That was all we needed to hear!" I still remember that whiskey: like a magic potion, sipped from an elf's jeweled flask, layer after layer of grassy, herbal spring freshness.

To be honest, the next batch I tried of it wasn't anywhere near as good. But that's part of craft distilling's wildly experimental designs, too. When you reach for the stars, sometimes you fall short. It's the ones that lift you out of your usual reality that make everything else worthwhile. What does exuberance add to the flavor of your whiskey? Anything!

The Russells tasting Wild Turkey in the warehouse.

"Perception Is Reality"

Lee Atwater was a brilliant American political strategist, something that has to be granted regardless of what you think of the people he worked for. Although Atwater died young, he left behind a legacy of political wisdom; and perhaps the brightest jewel in his hoard was this: "Perception is reality."

What it means is simple but deep. Atwater was saying that it didn't matter what reality, or the facts, actually were. What mattered was how people saw them. Before you dismiss this as the gimmickry of a political charlatan, remember that medical science backs him up by the admission of the placebo effect. Some medicines work because people think they're going to work, even when they're just sugar pills. Why should whiskey be any different?

If a whiskey is wrapped up in a fancy package, fancy words, or a top-shelf price, does that have an effect on the flavor? Several studies about the perceived price of wines suggest strongly that it does. If people perceive value in the package, they'll have a better opinion of the whiskey, often before they even try it.

I've seen it work in liquor stores. I've had whiskey makers admit it to me after they've redone packaging and seen sales (and positive comments) rise. If a new whiskey comes to market at a price that's equivalent to already well-regarded whiskeys of the same type, it stands a better chance of becoming well regarded itself.

You'll also see a general climb in prices when the collector's market pays an outlandish price at auction for a particularly rare or stunningly packaged bottle. The prices on that brand's entire line may well creep up, or even single malts in general. It's the "halo effect," where the reputation (or price) of an exceptional bottle at the top of the range draws all prices along with it.

The funny thing with pricing, though, is that there seems to be a different scale for craft whiskeys. Because of a lack of economies of scale, pressing debt service needs, or a simple struggle to keep the lights on, you may see a 2-year-old (or younger) craft whiskey priced the same as a 12-year-old bourbon or even a 15-year-old single malt. The craft whiskey will sell, even though it's often notably younger in flavor: perhaps hot, one-dimensional, over oaked from small barrels.

I suspect that there are a few different factors at play here, all relatively intangible. First, craft whiskey is more popular with people who are new to the category; either new to drinking beverage alcohol or new to drinking whiskey. They are referred to as "naïve drinkers," people who have very few preconceptions about what whiskey "should" taste like. If they try this new whiskey and it has flavors they like, that's exciting, and they'll stick with it.

There is also a "local hero" factor. Local producers are made much of these days—a trend I applaud, in general—and if a whiskey is made in your town or in your county, that's a plus. You'll be well disposed toward that whiskey and have a perhaps unrealized

tendency to give it the benefit of the doubt when it comes to critique.

Those days are changing as craft distillers get more experienced, and their whiskeys are better-crafted and can afford to have a bit more age on them. There are good craft-distilled bottled-in-bond 4-year-old bourbons that sell for less than twice as much as the bonded whiskeys from established distilleries, and that's a trend I'd like to see continue.

Packaging is another intangible that fits here. Does whiskey taste better when the bottle is heavy? Whiskey makers put corks in way too many bottles (in my opinion) when a good screw cap would make a better closure, simply because there's a perception that screw caps look cheap. "The good stuff always has a cork," one whiskey maker told me—and apparently everyone wants to be the good stuff.

Such signaling abounds in variety. Some whiskeys have a tube, either cardboard or metal, that the bottle sits in like a loaded torpedo, ready for launch. Molded bottles with waves of glass may imply that a whiskey has "marine" character, the brininess prized in some single malts. The Japanese Hibiki has a weighty bottle that has twenty-four facets, inspired by the twenty-four seasons of the Japanese calendar. Johnnie Walker isn't just packaged; it's color coded: from the workaday Red to the aspirational

Blue, with various colors, stoppers, and levels of trim in between.

What flavor is added by things like this? Packaging and other visual and tactile cues make the whiskey taste "better." Even I can still be led into that sometimes.

Am I saying it's true? It can be. When you approach a whiskey that you know is expensive, rare, elegantly packaged, or particularly old, it's natural to have expectations.

You can rely on your objectivity, you can rely on blind tasting (more on that in the next chapter), or you can simply enjoy the whiskey. After all, if all that stuff is combining to make the whiskey taste *better* to you, exactly who is being hurt in that transaction?

The Flip Side

*All of this works the other way as well, of course.
Put a great whiskey in a so-so package, and chances
are it won't receive as much love from the aficionados.
Why would a distiller want to do that?*

There are various reasons. For marketing reasons, a distiller will often want to have a whiskey to sell in every price range, and one way to put a whiskey in the lower price brackets is to bottle it with a plastic screw cap, maybe even in a plastic bottle, with a simply printed label.

That kind of packaging won't get a whiskey much love from the critics, but it sure does make friends with a lot of everyday drinkers. I have an admission: I regularly buy bourbon and rye bottled that way—and Irish whiskey, too. If you're a Canadian and ginger fan, you have plenty of choices in this range. Japanese whisky makers have them, too, though they can be hard to find outside of the home market.

Why does a "pro" whiskey drinker get the bottom-shelf stuff? It is because I like a tall highball of rye and ginger when I grill in the summer and because I have friends who feel the same way. This is a good way to drink whiskey when it's "just a drink," and that's the solution to a problem I've noticed with the serious

aficionado (or the aficionado who takes themself too seriously).

That problem is this: Some people don't seem to realize that whiskey does not have to be the focus every time you have a drink. My "first reader," Sam Komlenic, often comes by the house with some new whiskeys; and I'll offer some as well. We'll taste, compare, and discuss. But when that's done, we'll pour one for drinking; and the conversation immediately turns to local politics, history, and food.

If I'm just sitting out on the front porch with my dogs, watching the day go by, or if I'm reading a book on a cool night, likely as not there's a screw cap bottle of whiskey by my side, and maybe an ice bucket if it's a hot day. Screw cap whiskey tastes fine—if maybe not fantastic—which is perfect, because I've got other things on my mind.

 J. W. Dant Bonded

Poured from a screw-capped plastic bottle. Nose of allspice, cinnamon, and teaberry. Corn, oak, more teaberry-mint with solid heat into the finish.

Truth

There's one more thing that seems to have an effect on the flavor of whiskey in an intangible kind of way: the truth. I mean the truth about where a whiskey is made, which is not as obvious as it may seem.

"Sourced" whiskey has been part of the whiskey business for a very long time. Someone gets an idea for a whiskey, a particular flavor profile, or just a name and a story. They go to a distillery or a broker, and they figure out what barrels they have to buy to make their whiskey. If it sells or if they're optimistic enough to set it up in advance, they get more of the same kind of barrels. And then you have a branded whiskey with no actual physical distillery behind it.

Most blended Scotch whiskies are sourced from a number of different distilleries, not a single named distillery. Japanese blends are put together from different whiskies made within the company, but may also be made with imported bulk whisky from Scotland or Ireland: *caveat emptor*, because there's currently no legal requirement to note that on the label. There are major Canadian brands without owned distilleries. Until quite recently, Tullamore Dew didn't have a

distillery; it hadn't had one since the 1950s. Similarly Bulleit built a brand years before they built a distillery. These brands don't generally make a point of telling us where they come from.

Some whiskeys do, however. High West, Blaum Brothers, Belle Meade, Smooth Ambler, and others are pretty open about it. Bulleit openly acknowledges where they get their rye whiskey: the MGP facility in Indiana, the same as many other sourced brands. They tell the truth and shame the devil, as the old saying goes.

So what? Does it make a difference in how it tastes if you know where the whiskey comes from? Aficionados say they want transparency, and while some of them mean "I want to know every single detail about how you made this whiskey," most of them want to know *who* made it and *where* more than they want to know how.

To hear some people talk, the truth about these questions has more impact on the flavor than anything else. They learn that a whiskey isn't what they thought it was, and suddenly it doesn't taste as good, the price is too high, and they don't want anything more to do with it.

I don't need to know everything about a whiskey; I don't even need to know where it's from. All I ask of a sourced whiskey is that they're not lying to me about where it comes from. If a whiskey label, a whiskey brand, does consistently lie or misdirect about where it's made, who makes it, what part the people putting the label on the whiskey actually had to do with putting the flavor into the whiskey, then it does change the taste for me. It makes it taste like lies and disappointment, and I'll probably find another brand, even if this one was something I liked.

The truth is perhaps more intangible than any other thing that goes into a whiskey. But there's no denying its importance. Stick to the truth.

George Dickel Rye

Dickel tags Indiana's MGP as the source for their rye whiskey. Powerfully sweet nose with oak framing, and that's exactly what you get on the palate. And the truth leaves no distraction from doubt.

The Tasting

We've finally put your whiskey together. Every flavor input, from the huge contributions of the barrel and the warehouse to the tiny tweaks of the mash hydration and the milling of the grain, has been included. It's all sitting in the bottle on the bar in front of you, just waiting to be unleashed. Years of work have gone into it, the contributions of many people, places, and machines.

What are you waiting for? Let's take it out for a spin!

If you want to have a simple drink, maybe a tot at the end of the day or something to celebrate a win, it's likely that you'll want to snap open that cap, pour a generous amount into a glass or two, and relax in a comfy chair with your partner or friends nearby. Good whiskey! Turn up the music and let your mind roll on.

But if you really want to get everything you can possibly taste out of this whiskey, in this moment, it's going to take a little bit of work on your part. That's not really asking that much after all the effort everyone else put into it. Once you've done the work, you'll reap the benefits in the future. Concentrate and find those little hints of violets, or the licorice hiding behind the tarry rope, and you'll find them waiting the next time you open this bottle.

Chapter 16:

Framing the Tasting

You have to prepare to get the most out of a whiskey. Part of that is physical preparation. First clear your mouth and hands of any food or cooking aromas, and try to sample in an area free of such smells. Some of the master blenders won't eat food with garlic even two days before they're going to be sampling whiskey, though that's asking a lot from ordinary folks like us.

Next clear your perceptions of any other type of sensory distraction. Silence your phone; turn off the radio and television. If music helps you focus on other things, put some on. If it gets you singing along, turn it off for a while, since it's a good bet the whiskey is going to taste "better" because of it.

Get your glassware. I've made some suggestions in the sidebar.

If you can do a blind tasting, that's great. You'll find that not knowing what you're tasting will focus your senses tremendously. If that's not an option, there are benefits to an open-label tasting as well; you have context and a point of comparison. Don't worry about how you're tasting so much as what you're tasting.

Blind versus Open Tasting

Blind tasting doesn't require a blindfold, but it does require an assistant. You need at least two possible whiskeys to taste—more is better—and someone who can pick the whiskeys randomly and pour one or pour several and mark the glasses so the assistant knows which is which. Then you taste, record what you get from each whiskey, and only then have the assistant reveal what was in each glass.

What's the point? You may think you're able to taste a whiskey without prejudice, but you're not. It's because your brain is just too powerful. If you see a label or a distinctive bottle shape and you know what that whiskey is, your brain is already building expectations. You may think "Expensive whiskey! This will be great!" or "Cheap whiskey... boring," or "Ah, favorite whiskey— I love this." And you've already affected what you're going to taste and, by the way, cheated yourself out of a new experience.

At another level, if you're tasting for a competition, even something as simple as a local newspaper article about the "best local whiskey!" you want to protect the results from any taint of personal preference. I speak from sad experience: There's always someone out there who thinks a tasting is rigged. Do it blind and you've already greatly increased the confidence level about the results.

If you're feeling particularly objective, you can do a triangle test. Here your assistant has three different whiskeys and three glasses. Your assistant pours three samples and brings them to you—and the fun begins. Was it three different samples? Or two of Whiskey A and one of Whiskey C? Or maybe just three samples of Whiskey B? I've done triangle tests where I got two whiskeys and, unexpectedly, a brandy, and it threw me. Is there a lot of sherry cask influence here? What's all that vaporous fruit doing in my whiskey?

The point of blind tasting is to force you to focus directly on what you're smelling and tasting, and nothing else. Don't take into account the whiskey's name or reputation, the details of how it's made or where it's aged, or your own personal preferences. Just nose, taste, and linger with the whiskey, completely blind to anything else.

You can even get blue glassware to take the whiskey's color out of consideration.

Or turn it on its head and do an open-label tasting. Bring everything you know to bear on the whiskey: where it's made and who makes it and how, what you know about previous bottlings you've tried, what makes this one different. This will inform your experience more than a blind tasting can, and you'll look for what you know. Is it there? Is this a significant departure?

You can also do a tandem open-label tasting, comparing a new whiskey to a familiar one from the same maker or another.

I find these tastings to be very revealing. They will hone my focus almost as sharply as a blind tasting as I try to tease out every difference, so much so that my subjectivity gets left behind. This is a rewarding sampling method that can easily be done solo.

 ### The Glenlivet Enigma 2019

Details of this whisky were unrevealed when I wrote this; it's Glenlivet, but nothing else— age, cask, finish—was known. Sharp nose: malt, roasted corn, hard candies. Quite sweet palate, cocoa notes; seems like some sherry cask evidence. Can't wait to find out what it is!

That said, some folks still fear that they'll somehow "get it wrong" and not find what they're "supposed" to taste. Stop worrying, because every pro taster will come up with a different list of descriptors for a whiskey. That's simply how people work. As you get better, your list of scents and flavors will become more congruent with others. There will be some notes that every taster gets, but they will never be identical. That's the magic of self and the magic of whiskey. Taste it, write it, and move on.

To do that, you'll need some very simple equipment. Get a tumbler and some plain water, preferably not chilled. You may want an eyedropper or some kind of pipette to add small amounts of water to the whiskey when the time comes. Add some plain crackers or bread, something crusty, like a baguette. You'll want to clear your palate after each whiskey.

Get your note-taking setup: a pen and a notebook, a pencil and pad, a laptop or electronic tablet. You don't have to take notes, but I find that it helps me focus. Finally get a piece of white paper and tape it to a vertical surface. You'll be able to hold the whiskey up to the paper to get a better eye on what color it is.

Pour the whiskey (or, if you're blind tasting, have your assistant pour it and bring it to you). Settle yourself. Relax. It's whiskey time.

The Glencairn Glass

When I drink whiskey, I usually take it in an old-fashioned glass, the solid-based low tumbler used to build that classic cocktail. It's heavy in my hand and feels solid, there's room for ice if it's a hot day, and there's also room for the volatile aromas to bloom.

When I taste whiskey with attention and effort, I taste it from the Glencairn glass, the product of Glencairn Crystal, a Scottish family glass business. Its design is the result of consultation and trial with master blenders and distillers and is widely accepted in the industry.

Why do I use the Glencairn? At first it was because I had a lot of them. They were the glass of choice at almost all the early whiskey festivals, mainly because they were the first glass designed specifically for nosing and tasting whiskey. Before I knew it, I had over two dozen.

It is also a good idea to try whiskeys from the same glass to eliminate any variable that different glassware might create. I'm not much of a believer in the idea that "the right glass" can make whiskey (or wine or beer) taste better. But I do believe they can deaden or obscure flavors.

So why have I stuck with the Glencairn? It's comfortable and holds the right amount of whiskey. There's a solid little base to grip it, a bowl to hold the whiskey and let the volatile aromas come off and gather, and then the signature chimney that brings those aromas directly to your nose.

There are other whiskey tasting glasses that have come along, but the Glencairn has served me well for years, and I've seen no real reason to change after trying the others. I'd encourage you to try them all out and find your favorite.

Nose and Tongue

Before you taste the whiskey, you'll want to smell it. It only makes sense, because your nose is a much, much more sensitive organ than your tongue.

While your tongue can really separate only five flavor types—salt, sweet, sour, bitter, and *umami*, the last of which is a sort of richness—your nose is capable, after training, of identifying hundreds of thousands of aromas. Just think of how many aromas you can identify for bananas alone: ripe banana, underripe banana, overripe, cooked, burnt, thawed; the scent of the peel, of the butt (they are different), of a green peel. That's at least nine scents just for one fruit!

As we've been discussing, there are many ways that aroma can be created in whiskey. They put all that together in the bottle, and then it's your job to tease it apart.

So close your eyes, relax, and bring the glass to your nose. Don't jam your nose into it; that's a good way to beat up your olfactory nerves with alcohol. Instead hover: Hold your nose over the opening as you tilt the glass toward you, then move your nose from the bottom to top of the opening. You'll get the heavier, sweeter aromas sliding up and over the edge, then lighter, perhaps nutty aromas, and then any light floral or fresh fruit aromas escaping at the top. (We're assuming there are no off aromas in this ideal glass.)

Got that? Good. Now stick your nose in the crook of your elbow and take a deep sniff. This is an old taster's trick. You're essentially smelling yourself, the background aromas of sweat, perfume, laundry detergent that make up the smell you smell all day: your baseline. Smelling like that hits the reset button on your nose and sets you back to ground state, as it were.

Now smell the whiskey again, but take it easy. We've been talking about focusing your attention, but right now you want to let it wander. There's an episode of the celebrated crime drama *The Wire* where they talk about the idea of looking at a crime scene with "soft eyes," a deliberate unfocusing of attention that opens your mind to seeing things out of place or finding patterns that a sharp look won't find. You want to approach a new whiskey with a soft nose, not looking for anything in particular but just letting it happen to you.

As you do, you'll smell things that are either immediately familiar—molasses, orange, diesel smoke—or that might hang right on the edge of recognition: unspecified fruit, sweet, "spicy." Mull that over and see if any of them resolve. Look up one of the flavor wheels that are available on the web and see if the lists of descriptors jog a particular aroma for you: figs, maple, sawdust.

Don't smell too long or too deeply; you can overload your senses. Pause and think. Now try it again, this time with your mouth open, and breathing through both your nose and mouth. This engages the receptors in the connecting passages, and you may find more aromas coming to your attention.

Time to sip. You want to take a fairly small sip, spread it over your tongue, and swallow. The first one's really to get your tongue set up. Have some water. Now take another small sip and let it sit on your tongue for a few seconds. Roll it off your tongue and "chew" the whiskey, move it around in your mouth so it touches every part, and gently breathe in through pursed lips as you do it. This isn't just about tasting but about spreading the whiskey around on all the warm skin in your mouth to heat it and bring out the volatiles. Feel those flavors and the alcohol heat in your mouth, feel the creaminess, the tannic grip, the oaky dryness.

At this point, you're not just tasting; you're also smelling, deeply, as the volatiles rise through the back of your mouth and touch the olfactory receptors in the back of your nose. This is the richest, most effective way to experience your whiskey—with taste, touch, and smell combined. As the eighteenth-century French gastronome Jean-Anthelme Brillat-Savarin put it: "The taste and the sense of smell form but one sense, of which the mouth is the laboratory and the nose the chimney."

All the flavors and aromas that have been built into your whiskey are here, but you still may not be able to taste them. If you'll remember what we talked about in chapter 13 about proofing, sometimes the amount of water in a whiskey can hide or reveal flavors. Take your eyedropper (or carefully pour from a pitcher) and drop a small amount of water into the whiskey. Swirl it, have another sniff, and sip. You'll taste the whiskey differently now; some aromas move back or disappear, while others come to the fore. The heat will be less, and the "finish," the flavors and aromas that linger on the tongue after the swallow, will change as well.

Make your notes, have a few more sips, and sharpen your impressions. If you want, leave the whiskey for twenty minutes and come back to it: It will have changed again as it interacts with oxygen in your glass.

You've tasted the whiskey and all the flavors and aromas that took so long to develop and integrate. Now you can unlock them again any time you open the bottle.

Taste Everything

If you want to taste everything in a whiskey, I have some advice to pass on to you. It's from an interview with Kermit Lynch, the wine importer (and writer—get a copy of his fantastic book, **Adventures on the Wine Route**). *I don't have the exact text anymore, though I kept a copy for years; even Google can't recall it for me.*

Lynch said that you should pick a wine and learn everything you can about it: where it was made, what the countryside is like. Taste the grapes; ask who made the wine and how, what they're like and what other wines they make, how long wine's been made there, and what the other wines in the area are like. Then you will know that wine, and what it truly tastes like, better than you ever can by simply drinking a glass of juice.

Learn everything you can about a whiskey. Ask good questions and listen carefully to the answers. Travel to where it is made, walk the ground, watch the grain coming in, and smell that diffuse blanket of dusty sweetness. Enter the warehouses if you can and lay your hand on the barrels. Breathe deeply and take in that warehouse richness or the peat reek. Smell the hot fresh malt in the mash room on Speyside, the sweet funk of fermenting bourbon mash, the strangely fresh aroma of the brewery when they're making single pot still wash at Midleton. Feel the heat in the still room; hear the gush of water from any number of springs. Talk to the people who make it; hear their stories.

It has nothing to do with the flavor, seeing that, knowing that. It has everything to do with the enjoyment.

Enjoying the Best Whiskey

If you want to find the best whiskey, it's simple: Taste widely and decide what your favorite is.

There is no other way. You can't ask me (I don't even have a favorite!), you can't look at numeric ratings in magazines or online, and you certainly can't ask on a social media group: You'll get more opinions than there are whiskeys, and there are bound to be those that directly contradict each other.

Don't make up your mind too early. You'll only limit yourself, and that's never good. Don't let anyone else tell you "I only drink X whiskey; it's the best!" I realize that there are a staggering number of whiskeys, often with staggering prices. But these days you'll have to take the price into account when you're deciding what your favorite whiskeys are. Back in the late 1990s, when I started drinking whiskey for a living (and with a much more serious eye to flavor), whiskeys were substantially cheaper than they are now. There's nothing to be done about that outside of simply sighing for the good old days.

Don't fall into the error of putting too much credence into the online opinions of whiskey wowsers, either. They'll try to convince you that you have to spend a lot to get good whiskey, that popular whiskeys are trash, or that you need to constantly hunt for rare whiskeys. My friends, I do this for a living. I've tasted rare and wonderful whiskeys from all over. The whiskeys I drink most often all cost under $50 a bottle, most of them under $30. Start with the popular bottlings and take direction from there. Don't take your driving lessons in a Ferrari.

Take tasting opportunities where you can find them. Bars often host tastings that will offer flights of small pours at a fraction of the price you would pay by the drink. There are whiskey clubs that will share the cost of a high-end bottle and some that have members who like nothing better than buying one of those rare or expensive bottles and sharing it with folks who might otherwise never get so much as a sniff. Distillers often hold tasting events; get on their email lists and watch for one to come to your town.

When you've found some whiskeys you know you enjoy, expand your enjoyment by relaxing with them. Don't save them for a special occasion; make any occasion special by having a great whiskey! Relax about how you drink them. If you want some water in your whiskey, add it. If you want a cube or two of ice, drop it in. (I'd advise you to skip the whiskey stones; they're tough on the teeth, and I broke a glass with them once.) And by all means, if you want to make a highball in the summer— or the winter!—get out the ice and the soda and have at it! It's your whiskey; do what you want with it.

Of course, the best way to drink whiskey isn't neat, with ice, or in a cocktail. It's when you drink whiskey with friends, new or old. Whiskey shared is twice enjoyed, and there's just something positively conspiratorial about sharing whiskey, especially when you know other people aren't.

One of my favorite people in the industry, Wild Turkey Distilling Company's legendary master distiller Jimmy Russell, told me something long ago (and I'm sure he's told lots of people, as have I): "We don't really care how you drink it," he said, with a grin, "just so long as you drink it."

I like that, but I think I like this one even more. I'm not certain, but I believe I was talking to the incomparable Anthony Burnet, an early brand ambassador for Glenmorangie. We were talking about whisky collectors, and he shook his head, and said, "Take it off the shelf. We make it to drink."

That's what I'd like to leave you with. Remember: The only reason they make whiskey, and the only reason you have whiskey, is to drink it. Do that and savor every drop, every bit of flavor that's been packed into it in so many different ways.

Cheers!

Acknowledgments

When a person who's never distilled a drop of whiskey in their life writes a book about making whiskey, you know they had a lot of help.

Special thanks go to five guys at Ardbeg and Glenmorangie who were an immense help on this project. First of all, my deep thanks to Dr. Bill Lumsden. Not only did Dr. Bill answer a lot of dumb questions over the years, something he said inspired the idea of the book itself; so I blame him. His fellow blender, Brendan McCarron, often provided details to fill in Bill's broad brushstrokes. David Blackmore and Dan Crowell, Glenmorangie brand ambassadors, were a big help as well, both as conduits and as sources of information. Finally a hat tip to retired Glenmorangie brand ambassador Anthony Burnet, whose trenchant observations about whisky collecting still ring true today.

To the team at Buffalo Trace, my thanks for your continuing assistance, patience, and solid information: Mark Brown, Harlen Wheatley, Amy Preske Rose, Kristie Wooldridge, and the late Elmer T. Lee, Ronnie Eddins, and Truman Cox, three men who are sorely missed.

To the very patient and knowledgeable people who submitted to thorough questioning on stuff I just did not get: Stuart MacPherson of the Edrington Group, Connor O'Driscoll of Heaven Hill, Herman Mihalich of Dad's Hat, Ian Palmer of InchDairnie, Liz Rhoades of Diageo, Chris Morris of Brown-Forman, Greg Roshkowski of Brown-Forman Cooperage, Dr. Pat Heist of Wilderness Trail, chemists Bob Simpson and Scott Spolverino, Jay Erisman of New Riff, and Dr. Don Livermore of Wiser's.

There are a number of folks who have helped me over the past twenty-odd years, learning about whiskey and whiskey making, and as my parish priest always says on Christmas Eve, I apologize to the ones I know I forgot. Thanks to Richard Paterson, David Stewart, John Glaser, Jeff Arnett, Jimmy and Eddie Russell; Fred Noe and his father, the late Booker Noe; Jim Rutledge, Jerry Dalton, the late Parker Beam and his son Craig Beam, Dave Scheurich, Greg Davies, Bill and Rob Samuels, Andrew Mackay, Marianne Eaves, Denny Potter, Matt Hoffman, Bruce Joseph, Christian Krogstad, Alan Bishop, David Quinn, Colum Egan, Mike, Miyamoto, Paul Hletko, Rob Cassell, and sadly, the late Jim Swan.

Whiskey is a business, and there are folks in that business I owe gratitude to. Thanks to Joe Magliocco of Michter's, Robin Robinson, Frank Coleman and the crew at the Distilled Spirits Council of the U.S., Josh Hafer, Larry Kass, Lauren Cherry, Kylie Flett, Alexandra Clough, Monique Huston, the fabulous Mike Miller, Dave Schmier, John Cooper, Peter Mulryan, Fionnán O'Connor, and Ryan Maloney.

My colleagues, the whiskey writers and editors I work with, have taught me a lot, and I owe them. Thanks to Dave Broom, Chuck Cowdery, Wayne Curtis, Davin de Kergommeaux, John Hansell, Maggie Kimberl, Charlie MacLean, Johnny McCormick, Fred Minnick, Noah Rothbaum, Gavin Smith, Mike Veach, David Wondrich, Max Watman, Liza Weisstuch, and Jim Murray. Special thanks to Brian Ashcraft for help understanding Japanese whisky regulations.

I owe special thanks also to a couple of very good friends. Marty Duffy, the U.S. brand representative for the Glencairn Glass, has been my travel companion on a number of trips over the past few years as we did a fun series of whiskey presentations (with the droll Tom Johnson of the Aroma Academy).

Sam Komlenic isn't just a good friend and solid drinking buddy, he's also an authority on Pennsylvania distilling history and a stickler for proper grammar and punctuation, which has made him invaluable to me as my First Reader. Sam went over every word of this manuscript and caught a few embarrassing missteps. Thanks, Sam!

I do owe thanks to the people who got the book from my mind into your hands: my agent, Marilyn Allen, and my editor at Quarto, Thom O'Hearn. It's been a pleasure, thanks!

My family has always been a great support, and there is no way I could do it without them. My mother, Ruth; my children, Thomas and Nora; the dogs, Maud and Pippin. And my wife, my support, my strong heart, Cathy. You make it possible; you make it worthwhile.

Finally I dedicate the book to the memory of our beloved Corgi, Penderyn, who saved my life once. You're off the leash, little buddy. Chase those geese right up into the sky.

About the Author

Lew Bryson has been writing about beer and spirits full-time since 1995. He was the managing editor of Whisky Advocate *from 1996 through 2015. He is currently a Senior Drinks Writer for the Daily Beast, and also writes for Scotch Whisky. com, Artisan Spirit, and Bourbon+.*

Bryson is the author of *Tasting Whiskey* (Storey Publishing, 2014), a broad survey of the whiskeys of the world, their history and manufacture. He has also written four regional brewery guidebooks from Stackpole Books: Pennsylvania Breweries; New York Breweries; Virginia, Maryland & Delaware Breweries; and New Jersey Breweries (with Mark Haynie).

He was selected as the 2008 winner of the Michael Jackson Beer Journalism Award (Trade and Specialty Beer Media). He has served as a judge for both the American Craft Spirits Association and the Great American Beer Festival.

Lew Bryson lives north of Philadelphia with his wife and two Welsh Corgis.

Index